OUR PAINTED PAST
Wall Paintings of English Heritage

Caroline Babington, Tracy Mannin
and Sophie Stewart

D1344908

ACKNOWLEDGEMENTS

Our first thanks must go to David Park, Head of the Conservation of Wall Painting Department, Courtauld Institute of Art, for allowing us to draw on his extensive – and ongoing – research into English medieval wall paintings. We are also extremely indebted to Sharon Cather of the Courtauld, who kindly read the text and made many useful suggestions for improvement. Much of this book results from our extensive condition survey undertaken between 1993 and 1996, and we thank Jane Davies for her considerable involvement. At English Heritage, we are especially grateful to Robert Gowing of the Wall Painting Section for his patient coordination of the publication, Val Horsler for her tireless editorial help, and the designers Peta Morey and Pauline Hull for their work on the illustrations and design.

Contents

Foreword by Sir Jocelyn Stevens CVO   5

Introduction by Loyd Grossman   6

The English Heritage wall painting collection   7

Map of English Heritage sites with wall paintings   24

List of English Heritage sites with known wall paintings   25

Using this book   27

Greater London   28

South East   33

South West   43

East   53

East Midlands   61

West Midlands   64

Yorkshire & the Humber   65

North West   68

North East   70

Further reading   72

Opposite, detail from Westminster Abbey Chapter House

Published by English Heritage, 23 Savile Row, London W1X 1AB
Copyright © English Heritage 1999
Edited by Val Horsler
Designed by Pauline Hull
Printed in England by the colourhouse
ISBN 1 85074 751 2
A catalogue record for this publication is available from the British Library

Foreword

One of the more rewarding moments at English Heritage is the discovery of hitherto unknown aspects of a building's history. Nothing can be more dramatic than the discovery of a wall painting. When a face was seen peering from beneath a think growth of ivy at Berry Pomeroy Castle, and when the delicate faces of the Visitation emerged from beneath limewash at Chester Castle, all of us at English Heritage shared a collective intake of breath.

The wall paintings in the care of English Heritage are one of our greatest little-known treasures. Wall paintings – by definition inextricably part of the building in which they were made – provide a wonderful insight into our past. Even the simplest form of decoration can offer a wealth of information on the ways people once used historic buildings.

With 409 historic buildings in our care, we are responsible for one of the largest and most comprehensive collections of wall paintings in England, ranging from the painted niche at Lullingstone Roman Villa to the World War I graffiti in the detention cells at Richmond Castle. Twenty-five of our properties contain wall paintings of major national or international importance. Among these are the extensive 14th-century scheme in Westminster Abbey's Chapter House, the splendid 17th-century paintings in the Little Castle at Bolsover and the stunning medieval paintings in the Agricola Tower of Chester Castle.

English Heritage's expertise in caring for these treasures means that we are entrusted with the preservation not only of paintings in our own properties but also those in private ownership across the country. We provide a unique service advising on the condition, significance and importance of wall paintings throughout England, promoting research and training, and setting standards of practice and documentation. We are also the main source of funding for the care of wall paintings nationally, and the main source of advice on wall painting conservation for the Heritage Lottery Fund. Our direct involvement in numerous private projects has enabled us to develop conservation strategies and guidelines, and promote exemplary projects which underpin the advice that we give.

This book brings together the highlights of our collection for the first time - many of them previously unrecorded. As a group they form a fascinating testament to the history of England, and provide ample evidence of our continued commitment to the conservation of these fine works of art. I hope it will stimulate a renewed interest in England's spectacular painted heritage, a vital first step in its preservation.

Sir Jocelyn Stevens, CVO
Chairman, English Heritage

Opposite, detail from
St Mary's Church,
Studley Royal

Introduction

Detail from the 'Cupid and Psyche' mural, Hill Hall

G M Trevelyan wrote that 'The poetry of history lies in the quasi-miraculous fact that once on this earth, once on this familiar spot of ground, walked other men and women, as actual as we are today, thinking their own thoughts, swayed by their own passions, but now all gone, one generation vanishing into another, gone as utterly as we shall shortly be gone, like ghosts at cockcrow.' For anyone interested in the past as I am, the great moments come when you connect, however briefly, with those who worked, slept, prayed, celebrated, and suffered before us.

Our historic environment is made up of buildings, collections, and landscapes, but it is of course about people. In the Chapter House at Westminster Abbey, in the painted chamber at Cleeve, in the prisoners' cells at Richmond Castle you can look the past straight in the face thanks to our luckily preserved wall paintings. I say 'luckily' because they have had to survive through the religious and political upheavals of England's history. It is surprising, given the delicacy and beauty of the wall paintings you find in this book, that they do not have the widespread acclaim that their European counterparts enjoy.

This handbook to the wall paintings in our historic properties is published to coincide with English Heritage's first travelling exhibition devoted to the works of art in our care. I hope it will raise awareness of this marvellous resource and spread appreciation of a relatively unexplored aspect of 'the poetry of history'.

Loyd Grossman
Chairman, English Heritage Museums and Collections Advisory Committee

The English Heritage Wall Painting Collection

The wall paintings in English Heritage care – called a 'collection' but never deliberately put together – constitute a rich mixture of dates and styles, techniques and contexts. When viewed as a whole, they are typical of English wall paintings in general, though they have little more in common than the fact that they have all been painted directly on the building structure - be it stone, rubble, or plaster - making them as varied as the many historic buildings under the guardianship of English Heritage. Although our 'collection' may seem disparate, this is a reflection of the wide variety of contexts in which they are found, and the chance manner in which they have been preserved: by being covered, hidden, and forgotten.

We tend not to associate richly painted interiors with English buildings – as we would with other places such as Italy or France – but a tradition of wall painting has always existed in this country. We know this goes back at least as far as the Roman period: in fact, we have one Roman wall painting which survives in its original location, and countless fragments of such wall paintings which have been excavated from sites throughout England. Unfortunately, it is the result of catastrophic events such as the Reformation and an unusually early civil war that has all but sealed the fate of most of our wall paintings. Interestingly, although this has meant that more wall paintings were lost in England than in other European countries, it also makes English Heritage's collection all the more important. Most of our paintings survive because they were in castles and abbeys, precisely the artistic centres which would have held the finest works. Unlike churches and private homes which would have been used continuously, castles and abbeys were often abandoned and the paintings ignored. If one looks hard enough, an incredible amount can still be found, showing just how durable these wall paintings are.

We have to remember that many wall paintings were intended to be temporary; they were often covered over or repainted as dictated by fashion or changing tastes. Over the years English wall paintings have also changed in other ways. Because they cannot be separated from their environment and kept safely within museums, they are the most vulnerable form of painting. Not only are they susceptible to radical changes in building use, but the materials used to make them can change as well. The pigments may fade or darken, or even change colour completely, depending on environmental factors such as moisture or temperature, natural disasters such as fire or flood, or treatments by well-meaning restorers.

One of the most interesting aspects of wall paintings is what they reveal about their patrons and the way they used historic buildings, whether for worshipping, living, or entertaining. Our collection reflects this varied use of buildings in that our paintings survive in a myriad of contexts, including modest dwellings, religious settings, and stately homes. Their purpose may have been devotional, heraldic, decorative, or mythological, or they may even have just been graffiti. But because they are found today exactly where they were made, the visitor has the unique experience of seeing them in their original location, and perhaps, with a little imagination, understanding their original purpose.

Our wall paintings range in date from the Roman period to the 20th century, in technique from fresco to oil, in context from monastic to royal. They have been limewashed over, plastered over, encased in wood and stone, retouched and repainted. Yet in spite of all this, they have survived, and as their caretakers it is English Heritage's responsibility to ensure their safekeeping for future generations. In order to examine our collection it is helpful to group them according to context, and in this way a picture begins to emerge of a long-standing tradition in England for the painted interior. This is especially true of the Middle Ages, where the bulk of our collection lies.

The medieval wall paintings

DOMESTIC PAINTING

Our medieval paintings are particularly interesting for the unusual amount and quality of domestic paintings, which are fascinating evidence of contemporary taste and fashion. It was ultimately the patron, not the painter, who determined the location of the painting, the quality and cost of materials, and the subject matter. In the Middle Ages, the interiors of fine homes were always painted. The wealthiest patrons, such as those in royal households, augmented this with the use of tapestries or painted wall hangings (a more expensive, and more portable version of wall paintings) to add warmth or decoration for special occasions. Indeed, as the vast majority of these cloth hangings have perished over time, wall paintings often provide the only evidence of what these may have been like.

A fine example of a fully-painted medieval interior, unique in England for its almost complete survival, is the internationally important Great Tower at Longthorpe, Cambridgeshire which dates to the early 14th century. Where usually only fragments remain, at Longthorpe an extensive scheme survives on all of the walls, windows, and vaults. Although these are a rare survival, the patrons in this case were not particularly unusual or grand, so it seems that wall paintings like this may have been more common than we realise. This is all the more remarkable when we look at the extraordinary subject matter found at Longthorpe, described as a 'spiritual encyclopaedia' with biblical, moral, didactic, and secular subjects largely derived from contemporary literature. Several extremely rare subjects are included, for example the Wheel of Senses with each sense represented symbolically, a subject whose only parallel is a 13th-century painting at the abbey of Tre Fontane near Rome.

While there is an extraordinary range of subject matter at Longthorpe, the inclusion of religious subject matter in a domestic setting was not at all uncommon. A fine contemporary parallel was recently discovered at Fiddleford Manor in Dorset. The painting, in the Solar, depicts an Annunciation flanking the central window. The arrangement of the Annunciation on either side of a window opening is reasonably typical and is found, for example, as far afield as the Arena Chapel, Padua, and Prior Crauden's Chapel, Ely, both from the 14th century.

Interior of Longthorpe Tower

Although certainly a high-quality building, Fiddleford was only a modest manor house, unlike such grand buildings as Stokesay and Belsay, which also contain fragments of 14th-century domestic painting. These were essentially fortified manor houses, both formidable and even militaristic in appearance, very much designed to protect the occupants against attack. Yet at the same time they were homes, and the wall paintings are evidence of the value placed on comfortable surroundings.

The 14th-century painted foliage pattern in the Buttery at Stokesay, one of the finest surviving manor houses in England, is one of the few examples we have of purely decorative domestic medieval painting. The decoration is fairly simple, consisting of a curving red leafy vine pattern – sometimes called scrollwork – on a plain white background. However, this room was clearly designed as a service area, a location which under normal circumstances would never have been decorated in this way. This indicates that at some stage the use of this room must have changed dramatically, even if only temporarily.

Of similar date is the fine painted scrollwork which survives in the Great Hall at Belsay Castle. Here, the paintings appear to be evidence of the earliest decoration of the castle, and therefore also date from the 14th century. However, the paintings at Belsay are complicated by the fact that a later scheme of decoration was painted directly over them in the 15th century, no doubt as a result of changing fashion. Not only does this make the interpretation of both schemes more difficult, but it can cause problems when attempting to conserve them. Both schemes are equally worthy of preservation, both are important examples of domestic decoration from two different periods, and each one must be stabilised without compromising the other.

MONASTIC PAINTING

As we have seen in the wall paintings at Longthorpe Tower, relatively ordinary settings could be treated very elaborately, using a sophisticated range of pictorial references. However, domestic decoration does not end with secular buildings. In the care of English Heritage there are 16 medieval abbeys and six medieval priories which contain wall paintings in their living quarters. The differences in the style, amount, and quality of the decoration appear to have been dictated by the monastic order, which in our collection include Cistercian, Premonstratensian, Augustinian, Benedictine, Dominican, Franciscan, and Cluniac. The majority of these paintings date to the early 13th and 14th centuries, with the exception of two of the priories (Brinkburn and Tynemouth) which only retain post-medieval decoration.

Although many abbeys and priories used very simple decorative motifs, the lavishness and expense of the painted decoration could vary greatly. An example of the type of paintings at the absolute top end of the scale are the fabulous wall paintings at Westminster Chapter House. These date to the 1380s, and were equal to anything painted in Europe at the time.

The paintings at Westminster depict the Last Judgement and the Apocalypse of St John, and are of extremely high quality. The fine brushwork is very skilled, allowing for great detail, and there is extensive use of expensive pigments, gold and silver leaf, and modelled plaster additions that give the impression of attached jewels. Indeed, the quality of the work matches the importance of the location – the chamber was used for the monks' assemblies, as well as secular council meetings, and was an occasional meeting place for the House of Commons. Even more exciting is the fact that we know who commissioned them – a monk at Westminster Abbey – and that they were clearly meant as part of an entire decorative ensemble which would have been truly magnificent, including painted sculpture, spectacular stained glass windows, and a tiled floor. What is remarkable is that, even here, in one of the most important abbeys in one of the most

Interior of Westminster Abbey Chapter House

important artistic centres in Europe, the Chapter House could not escape change: the use of the room has been altered radically over the years, from Chapter House to House of Commons, to Record Office, and finally back to Chapter House in the 19th-century restoration. It is remarkable that the paintings have survived, although their appearance today is a direct result of such a chequered history.

Although these extraordinary paintings now seem to stand alone in the history of monastic English wall painting, this is not the case. Fragments of highly sophisticated medieval wall paintings survive in other English Heritage abbeys and priories, giving us an idea of what once existed at these sites. One of the most exciting of these is the recently identified 14th-century Virgin and Child in the chancel of the Prior's Chapel at Castle Acre Priory, Norfolk. At Greyfriars Abbey, Great Yarmouth, there are remains of an exquisite depiction of a female figure, dating to the early 14th century, at the back of a tomb recess. And at St Augustine's, Canterbury, which is the oldest of the abbeys, dating to 598, there are traces of a 14th century medallion pattern on the north side of the crypt chapel, a unique survival at this extremely important site.

Many of our abbeys are now ruined and exposed to the elements – which means that the paintwork tends to be fragmentary – but there is clearly a uniformity in the motifs and decoration chosen. Here and there tiny clues survive, sometimes only a square inch of painting, enabling us to imagine the original appearance of the interior. Fragments of wall painting, especially in partly ruined sites, tend to survive in protected areas such as niches, windows, and corners. Their discovery is often surprising, as with the well-preserved red-line

masonry pattern inside the Cloister book cupboards at Hailes Abbey, or within the tomb recesses of Easby Abbey.

The majority of the monasteries in English Heritage care – spanning the length of England from Cumbria to Somerset – are Cistercian, which is particularly significant as all forms of luxury and ornament were forbidden to this order. The main decoration found in the Cistercian abbeys – and there are traces at Roche, Byland, Waverley, and Cleeve – is single-line masonry pattern, painted in red, black, or white, with the simplest of pigments, or just incised with a sharp tool. The simplest decoration tends to be the earliest in date, usually dating to the early 13th century. The double-line masonry pattern found, for instance, in the Chapter House vestibule at Furness, or the library window splays at Cleeve, is generally later, dating to somewhere around the early 14th century.

Sometimes this ornament is embellished with leaves or rosettes, and a delightful example of this can be found in the piscina of the Sacristy at Cleeve Abbey. In a remote corner of Somerset, Cleeve is the most remarkable of our Cistercian abbeys because of the extraordinary amount of decoration that survives there. It really is exceptional: not only are there extensive remains of all the decorative types described above, but a large-scale figurative painting survives in a room known as the Painted Chamber. Dating from the 16th century, it was painted at a time when strict adherence to the Cistercian Rule was in decline, and is considered by experts to be the most significant late Cistercian wall painting in Britain. Similar to the fragments found at Castle Acre Priory, it shows the relative sumptuousness of the private rooms of the abbots and priors, reflecting a growing decadence towards the close of the Middle Ages.

CHURCH PAINTING

Apart from monasteries, there are four private castle chapels with medieval wall paintings in English Heritage care at Chester, Farleigh Hungerford, Berry Pomeroy, and Goodrich Castles. There is only one church in the collection that contains medieval decoration, the small isolated site of St Mary's, Kempley, in Gloucestershire.

The justifiably famous paintings at Kempley are by far the earliest of the group and form one of the most impressive Romanesque schemes in England. The first scheme of paintings, in the chancel and nave, date from 1130-40 and were discovered in the 1870s by the local vicar, who set about uncovering them in fairly amateur fashion. Although the paintings were damaged as a result, what survives is truly magnificent. Of international importance, the paintings comprise an Apocalypse scheme in the chancel, with rows of seated apostles who look up towards a splendid Christ in Majesty painted on the low barrel vault. Standing bishops and pilgrims complete the scheme at the east end, and provide tantalising evidence of who may have commissioned the paintings. The scheme continues on the east wall of the nave (the chancel arch) where in the Middle Ages a large sculptured rood, or crucifix, would have hung. The paintings here include a rare depiction of the Three Maries at the Sepulchre, identified only recently. And as if all of this were not enough, there are more traces of 12th-century painting in the nave, and important remains of several later schemes of decoration dating from

Interior of St Mary's Church, Kempley

the 14th to the 17th centuries, often overlapping each other, making this the perfect example of an English parish church with a long tradition of wall painting, and without doubt the finest example of medieval church painting in English Heritage care.

Kempley is unique in our collection in that it was a parish church; most of our church painting survives in what were private castle chapels. The earliest of these is the recently rediscovered scheme in the Agricola Tower (once the gatehouse) at Chester Castle, certainly one of the most important finds of recent years. The rediscovery of these paintings is typical of what often happened to wall paintings: the paintings were obscured, then forgotten, and only vague pictorial references testified to their existence. It was during the National Survey of Medieval Wall Painting in 1980 that busts of angels in roundels were discerned in the altar recess, which led to an investigation of the vault spaces. By gently thinning the limewash thereby rendering it transparent a beautiful image emerged of two female figures embracing, clearly a representation of the Visitation. The style of the paintings, extremely delicate and of very high quality, is considered similar in style to mid 13th-century sculpture at Westminster Abbey. The fact that both Westminster and Chester Castle were under the patronage of Henry III at the time raises the exciting prospect that the wall paintings could have formed part of a royal scheme of decoration. No other royal paintings survive from the 13th century except some small fragments at Windsor Castle.

Another equally dramatic discovery of a chapel wall painting was made in the 1980s at Berry Pomeroy Castle. The gatehouse at Berry Pomeroy was essentially a ruin which was completely enshrouded in thick moss and ivy; it was only when a workman at the castle noticed a face peering out from behind the vegetation that experts were called in and the painting was uncovered. It was found to be a stunning depiction of the Adoration of the Magi, dating to about 1500.

Post-medieval wall paintings

Unlike the medieval paintings in English Heritage care, which seem to form a coherent group when viewed as a whole, the post-medieval wall paintings are fewer in number, and the examples are more isolated. Clearly the Reformation, which spurred the dissolution of the monasteries and obliteration of religious imagery, had a catastrophic effect on the survival of our medieval wall paintings. Although many did not survive, we are fortunate that some were simply covered over. Moreover, this does not mean that wall painting then ceased; in fact it seems to have been funnelled into private contexts, and religious imagery appeared sporadically when private funding allowed.

One of the true highlights of our post-medieval collection is the Elizabethan cycle of paintings at Hill Hall, Essex. The unusual mixture of biblical and classical themes at Hill Hall has led to the suggestion that these stories may have been chosen specifically by the patron. They appear to be largely based on engravings and woodcuts which would have been widely available in the 16th century, and are unique in England for their extent and sophistication. Whether these paintings were executed by a foreign artist is unknown, but, as in the extensive scheme of 17th-century painting at Bolsover Little Castle, this is a distinct possibility. At Bolsover, we see a growing trend toward the Baroque style, introduced in England on a lesser scale by French artists coming from the court of Louis XIV.

In the 18th century, the Baroque tradition persisted, as we can see in the flamboyant painted ceilings of Chiswick House and the Archer Pavilion at Wrest Park. Both of these buildings have no particular purpose. They were designed for recreation, not living, and the paintings very much reflect this more light-hearted, less didactic, approach to interiors. There is extensive use of trompe l'oeil work in order to give an illusion of space, open skies, or classical architecture, in bright colours often with extensive gilding.

By the 19th century, we can see a radical change in the approach to domestic interiors. In the Drawing Room at Brodsworth Hall, the ceiling has been painted and gilded but the design is more rigid and formalised, with extensive use of stencils and repetitive motifs. At the other end of High Victorian style, however, is another one of the few churches in English Heritage care, the chapel at St Mary's, Studley Royal. This is a prime example of Victorian Gothic, where a workshop approach was used to decorate every inch of available space, including stained glass, mosaics, and painted stone, timber, canvas, and metal. These two very different examples from our collection, interestingly, reflect Victorian taste: as a rule they were extremely well-informed and would use a wide range of pictorial references, be it Baroque ceiling or medieval church, adjusting them to their own particular purpose.

An almost unique example of 19th-century wall painting is found at Osborne House, Isle of Wight. On display here is the one 'true fresco' of our collection, painted by the leader of the 19th-century fresco revival, William Dyce. Dyce was commissioned by Prince Albert in 1847 to paint a fresco on the Nursery Landing which, as a bold piece of history painting, hardly seems suited to a nursery setting. Indeed, Queen Victoria is reported to have worried about the nudity, but Prince Albert was so fascinated with the process of

Interior view of the central hall and side room of the Archer Pavilion, Wrest Park

fresco painting that he reportedly infuriated the artist with his offers of help.

And finally, our two examples from the 20th century both relate to the World Wars. The first is a poignant record left by prisoners of conscience imprisoned in a bleak cell block at Richmond Castle during World War I. Religious tracts, poems, and drawings were pencilled onto the limewash walls. These are very personal records, with the walls being treated almost like a diary. The second dates to World War II, and is a far more light-hearted piece. Soldiers stationed at Hurst Castle clearly needed entertainment, and so the west wing of the battery was converted into a theatre. The concrete walls of the gun battery make a distinctly odd backdrop to this romantic painting. In both cases the visual marks left by those caught up in the two World Wars bring it all very much to life.

The techniques of wall painting

THE PAINTERS' METHODS

Although one of the most tantalising features of English wall paintings is that we rarely know who painted them, our rich documentary sources give us some names, lists of materials, and costs which begin to allow a picture to emerge of the medieval wall painter. Contrary to popular belief, the painters were not monks but professionals, many of them associated with the more important monastic and political centres, such as the royal painters at Westminster whose work we see at the Abbey Chapter House, at Windsor, and possibly at Chester. Peterborough Cathedral was another centre which, given the connections of the owners of Longthorpe with the cathedral, tempts us to imagine that the painters came from there. Many of them came, or were summoned, from abroad for specific commissions, but there would also have been groups of travelling painters who undertook more modest commissions for houses and local churches.

It is fascinating as well as rewarding to unravel the working methods and materials of the medieval wall painter, since even the earliest paintings have been found to be extremely sophisticated. This study is vital because it can be easy to overlook these often damaged and fragmentary works, which are sometimes crudely over-painted or restored. More important, however, is the fact that such study informs our treatment of the paintings. So often in the past well-intentioned restorations have backfired because of mistaken assumptions about the techniques of wall painting.

SOURCES OF INFORMATION

We have a surprising amount of documentation on medieval painting techniques, and even a couple of instances where both the wall paintings and the original accounts for them survive. The best source is probably the royal accounts. Both Henry III and Edward III seem to have employed large numbers of painters and craftsmen for the palaces at Westminster, Windsor, and Clarendon, among others. Their names and salaries, the materials they used, and even the type of paint brushes they had are all listed in the *Liberate* and *Close Rolls*.

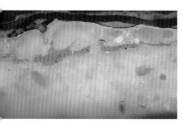

Right, figure from Westminster Abbey Chapter House; above, paint sample from the figure, showing gilding

Below, detail from Windsor Castle, King John's Tower

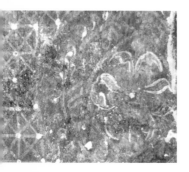

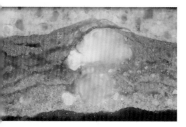

Above, paint sample from Windsor showing the build up of paint layers

All paint samples (pages 16–19) are photographed in cross-section at 200x magnification under light-polarising microscope

The accounts, for example, tell us that the wall paintings at Westminster Abbey Chapter House were commissioned by Brother John of Northampton, and that the Apocalypse painting cost £4 10s. They also led to a major discovery at King John's Tower, Windsor Castle, where wall paintings – which were thought to have been destroyed – were revealed under panelling during a recent refurbishment. This scheme consists of a wonderfully intricate pattern of brilliant emerald-green lozenges decorated with a delicate rose pattern, against a contrasting deep crimson star-covered background. The documentation is particularly detailed for these paintings, and we learn from the royal accounts of 1365-6 that the chief painter was William Burdon, who was paid a shilling a day for almost four months' work, and that he had five assistants working for slightly smaller sums of money. This number of people immediately indicates that a large, organised work-shop system was in place. From the pigments listed it is also clear that this was an extremely costly decorative scheme, using materials such as gold, blue bice (a manufactured copper blue), and vermilion. We also know that the painting was executed in oil and coated with two different grades of varnish.

As well as these primary sources, there are several early treatises on the subject, such as those written by Theophilus in the 12th century and Cennini in the 14th century. Both are very informative regarding pigment manufacture, and their recipes are quite useable. They offer a wealth of information on all aspects of painting technique, from grinding pigments to preparing varnishes, and give us invaluable insight into the working practices of the medieval painter.

Our knowledge has recently been considerably enhanced by the development of analytical techniques for wall paintings. To state the obvious, the problem with wall paintings is that they cannot be brought into the laboratory. Nonetheless, much can be learnt through analysis of microscopic paint samples using standard analytical techniques such as scanning electron microscopy (SEM) to identify pigments or Fourier transform infrared microspectroscopy (FTIR) for binding agents. On site, the use of different light sources to examine a painting, such as raking (sharply angled) light, ultraviolet, or infrared, can also yield interesting information on preparatory techniques and the presence of any later retouching or coatings. A recent development at English Heritage has been the use of video microscopy to examine a wall painting *in situ*.

PREPARATION OF THE PAINTING SURFACE

Much, however, can be gleaned from visual observation alone. The preparation of the ground for the painting was often remarkably rudimentary, consisting of nothing more than a coarse limewash skim over stonework, or an undulating plaster over a rough rubble support. In most cases little effort was made to smooth out trowel marks or obtain a flat surface finish in preparation for painting. However, this was often deliberate: the medieval painter usually avoided smooth surfaces in order to reduce reflection, making the paintings easier to see.

If the support was extremely uneven, it was usually plastered. The sequence of the plastering and the planning of the composition can frequently be detected, as in the Romanesque scheme at Kempley. The horizontal bands seen on the plaster in the chancel appear to correspond to scaffolding levels, and may indicate where the plasterer finished one day's work and started the next. Again, 100 years later, at Chester, plaster joins can be seen between the upper and lower register of scenes on the walls. Also of interest here is evidence of the way the scheme was laid out: there are holes made by compass points to draw the roundels in the altar recess, and traces of 'snap lines' on the plaster, where a string was snapped into the fresh plaster to mark out compositional divisions.

At this point it may be useful to clarify one of the major areas of confusion regarding the technique of English wall paintings. In general, they were painted on dry plaster or limewash using lime or other materials as binding agents. At Kempley and Chester, plaster joins and 'snap lines' have often been cited as evidence of fresco technique, that is where pigments are painted on to freshly applied sections of plaster, so that the paint becomes bonded to the surface by a process of carbonation. This method requires the painting to be completed quickly, before the plaster sets (hence the term *giornata*, or day-work, for each area of plaster), and the use of certain chemically stable pigments. At Kempley and Chester, however, the plaster patches are too large to have been completed in one day, and moreover the pigments used are often not compatible with true fresco technique. What is more likely in these cases, together with a handful of other paintings in England, is that work began

on the fresh plaster, and, in keeping with northern European practice, the paintings were reworked and altered using *secco* techniques. *Secco* – which means dry – is a term used for painting carried out on a dry surface or on plaster that has already set. In order for the paint to adhere to the surface a binder – or medium – must be used, and this could be one of a variety of organic materials such as oil, egg, or animal glue. In fact it is unlikely that there were any genuine frescoes in England before the 19th-century fresco revival.

DRAWING AND PREPARATORY TECHNIQUES

Little evidence survives of preparatory techniques, but occasionally they can be detected. Even the most skilled artists would have had to plot out their composition before beginning work – especially as wall paintings are on such a large scale – and there were many ways of doing this. The simplest method was to sketch the composition directly on to the wall using dilute pigment or charcoal. In the paintings at Berry Pomeroy, we find black outlining showing through abraded areas of the painting. At St Leonard's chapel, Farleigh Hungerford, there is also black underdrawing, but this is over a more sophisticated priming of two types of red paint. Then again, a drawing could be incised into the surface using a pointed instrument, either directly on to fresh plaster or indirectly by outlining over a full-size sketch on paper. Such a drawing – called a 'cartoon' – could be used in one of two ways. Either holes could be pricked in the paper, following the lines of the drawing, and, with the cartoon held against the wall, the drawing transferred to the wall surface by rubbing a small pouch of powdered pigment across the surface – a technique called 'pouncing'.

Above, one of the apostles in the chancel of St Mary's Church, Kempley; plaster joins are visible in raking light

Below, detail from the fresco by William Dyce at Osborne House, in normal and raking light, showing the presence of incisions made through a cartoon into wet plaster

Above, incised lines are visible in the Wheel of Life at St Mary's, Kempley, when viewed in raking light

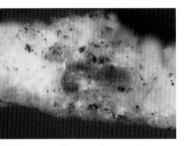

Above, paint sample from the 'blue' colour at St Botolph's church, Hardham, showing the black and white pigment mixture

Right, one of the blackened faces at Longthorpe Tower

Or the cartoon could be placed against the damp plaster and the design carefully traced with a blunt instrument, thus leaving an impression of the image on the wall. The first technique can be seen in some parts of the Drawing Room ceiling at Brodsworth Hall, and the latter technique is clearly visible in the fresco painting by William Dyce at Osborne House.

Sometimes these methods can appear surprisingly crude. At St Mary's Church, Kempley, for example, in the 14th-century scheme within the Wheel of Life, deep incisions mark out the wheel as well as each circular motif, probably made with some form of makeshift compass. At Longthorpe Tower the incised drawing is more delicate, with a rosette and the Wheel of the Senses neatly outlined. Often much of what we see is actually the preparatory drawing, because of hasty uncovering techniques or excessively harsh conservation treatments. This is certainly the case at Longthorpe Tower, where the final paint surface was substantially lost during uncovering in the 1940s.

Presumably the artist must have prepared small-scale sketches to show the patron for approval before beginning on the wall, but these rarely survive. How much planning was done in advance and how much was done on the wall itself remain a mystery. On occasions the final painting may vary quite considerably from the underlying drawing. Such last-minute changes made to a painting are known as *pentimenti* and are only visible under very close examination. The existence of *pentimenti* may indicate that the artist had deliberately decided to change elements of the scheme or that he was using the initial sketch merely as a rough guide. This rethinking is clearly visible in the repositioning of the background hills at Berry Pomeroy and in the figure drawing at Longthorpe Tower.

PIGMENTS AND MEDIA

Even from the earliest date, expensive and rare pigments were employed. In the Romanesque scheme at Kempley, for example, malachite and azurite, natural copper minerals, have been found in addition to a basic palette of red and yellow ochre, lime white, and black. The discovery of azurite at Kempley is very significant as this is the earliest known use in English wall paintings. There were English sources for these pigments, but the medieval writers frequently refer to azurite as German azure, which suggests that it was imported. For high quality work at this date, the even more expensive ultramarine (lapis lazuli) was used. This was probably imported from as far away as Afghanistan and has been found in contemporary painting in

Canterbury and Durham Cathedrals, and at the small parish church of Ickleton, Cambridgeshire.

Though not all paintings of this date had such generous budgets, a skilful painter could disguise this fact well. A good blue was always a problem for the early medieval painter, as the best colours were expensive to source and complex to manufacture. Analysis has revealed that a certain amount of optical trickery was used to get round this problem. It was found that if white and black were mixed in the right proportions, the result was a bluish effect (a phenomenon known as Rayleigh scattering). This technique was used in the earliest paintings, such as those at Hardham and Coombes churches in Sussex, dating to around 1100.

The later medieval paintings show an increasing richness in the range of pigments used. Those in St Leonard's chapel, Farleigh Hungerford, are made up of an extraordinary variety of pigments including orpiment (a very rare and unstable yellow pigment), lead-tin yellow, copper green, vermilion, red lead, and translucent glazes over gold and silver leaf. Metal foils have also been found at Westminster Chapter House and Greyfriars Abbey (both 14th century), and were used extensively in much later schemes such as those in Chiswick House (18th century) and Studley Royal (19th century). These were often painted with toned glazes in order to make silver appear gold, and to make gold more intense.

The identification of pigments in early paintings can be difficult because of the instability of some of them. With the exception of ochre, lime white, and black, most are affected by light or moisture, and over time may undergo a complete chemical alteration. For example, blue may become green (azurite converts to malachite in the presence of water), glazes may

fade, and white lead, red lead, and vermilion may blacken. These processes can be extremely complex, are not entirely understood, and can lead to misunderstanding of the original technique. For example, at Berry Pomeroy, a whitish veil was noted over parts of the Adoration of the Magi. Analysis showed this white to be an alteration product of red lead (cerussite), and therefore part of the original paint layer and not something to be removed. Another example is the blackened faces so often seen in early paintings, such as those at Longthorpe Tower. There was a theory that this was a black underpainting or a preparatory layer for the final painting, but again analysis has shown that the lead white has simply converted to black (plattnerite) over time.

Perhaps the most confusing area of all is the question of media. We know that a range of organic media including egg, oil, and animal glue were used to bind the pigments, and that inorganic media such as lime, or even the fresco technique, could be employed. The problem is that media analysis is very complex, and organic media can deteriorate to a point where they are virtually undetectable. This is further

Above and top, paint sample in cross-section from the garter of St George, Farleigh Hungerford, with gold leaf visible on the surface

Left, detail from the Adoration of the Magi, Berry Pomeroy, showing pentimenti; below, paint sample from Berry Pomeroy stained with a microchemical test for lead which revealed that the whitish 'veil' over the painting was an alteration product of lead

complicated by the fact that a combination of several types of binding medium could be used, and any coating applied later can confuse the evidence. The original choice of pigments often provides the best clues. For instance, lead- and copper-based pigments, and glazes, cannot be applied with lime or in fresco technique. The medieval accounts for Windsor and Westminster record quantities of oil, which indeed was a popular medium from very early on. Known on the continent from *c*900, the earliest example of the use of oil that we are aware of in England is at St Gabriel's Chapel (*c*1120), Canterbury Cathedral. Another important early example is the mid 13th-century wall paintings in St Faith's

St Faith's Priory, Horsham
St Faith's, Norfolk

Priory, Norfolk, where linseed oil has been identified.

By the 17th century, wall paintings were predominantly painted in oil on plaster, as at Bolsover Castle, with oil often used to seal the plaster as well as bind each of the pigments.

Towards the middle of the 19th century, there was extensive experimentation with complex recipes including the addition of resins, gums, and waxes to oil in order to increase its workability and durability. However, by the late 19th century, there was a renewed interest in monumental painting, and therefore true fresco technique, which focused on the redecoration of the Palace of Westminster. However, while Victorian painters became quite proficient in the technique, they tended to apply large amounts of detail after the initial fresco painting had set. The technique of Dyce's fresco of 'Neptune' at Osborne House typifies fresco painting of the period. A special support was designed, using laths and perpendicular wooden battens with air vents in order to protect the painting from moisture. Otherwise it is painted in true fresco technique, except for two pigments applied later with an organic medium. Although this painting survives in very good condition, in many of the works at Westminster the artists (including Dyce) were not so rigorous and altered the technique too much, causing the rapid and conspicuous deterioration of many of the paintings.

APPLIED ORNAMENT FOR WALL PAINTINGS

Wall paintings were often embellished with applied ornaments to enrich the painted surface. At Westminster Chapter House, gesso was used to model crowns and jewels, which were then painted and gilded. Also at Westminster, real parchment was used, inscribed with text, and simply glued to the wall surface. Attachments could also be made out of unusual materials: in the 17th-century Rycote chapel, gilded stars were fashioned out of old playing cards and fixed to the painted ceilings. In the 19th century, techniques became even more complex. As we can see at Studley Royal, entire paintings were executed on canvas in the studio and then glued to the wall surface. This reflects a general tendency at the close of the century away from monumental wall painting *in situ*.

Star-shaped cutouts from the Minstrel's Gallery, Rycote Chapel

The conservation of wall paintings

It was not until fairly recently that the formal discipline of wall painting conservation as a specialist profession began to be recognised. Previously, most of the work carried out involved artists and craftsmen, and although highly skilled, their treatment often focused around the visual or cosmetic improvement and restoration of the paintings. Prompted by the start of the Royal Commission survey of English medieval wall paintings in the 1980s, it became increasingly clear that the complex issues raised by wall paintings required specific consideration, and a programme of training in wall painting conservation was started at the Courtauld Institute in London. This programme, the first of its kind in the UK, focused on the determination and assessment of causes of deterioration, and the development of methods involving minimal intervention.

Within English Heritage too there has been substantial progress in understanding the history and condition of our own paintings and the development of approaches to their care. Most significantly, a comprehensive audit of our wall paintings was begun in 1994. Cataloguing the conservation history is fundamental to the understanding of the present condition of the paintings, and to the interpretation of both the causes and rate of decay. Many of our paintings appear to be in perilous condition, often exposed on ruinous sites, yet examination of their condition over time shows remarkably little change or loss. Our audit – which is ongoing – has provided English Heritage with the information required to prioritise conservation for those paintings that are truly in need, and to highlight others for which further recording, monitoring, and detailed research are necessary.

The results of the audit were also remarkable in the many new discoveries made, such as the fragments of wall painting at Castle Acre Priory and Goodrich Castle, and the development of previously unrecorded regional characteristics. For example, our northern collection is far more fragmentary than elsewhere, which may result from the fact that in the 19th century the fashion for stripping walls to the bare stone was especially popular in the north where the stone was of good quality.

Varying approaches are needed to tackle the needs of this very diverse collection, and the coordination of the treatment and monitoring of our wall paintings is very much an ongoing process, since by their nature wall paintings are always deteriorating. The chilling prison block at Richmond Castle, for example, with its historic graffiti by prisoners of conscience in World War I, is too fragile to be put on display, and the emphasis has been placed on recording

A conservator examining fragments of painting at Chester Castle using a video microscope

the drawings and stabilising their surrounding environment. A rather different case is the monumental scheme of paintings in the Little Castle at Bolsover. Forming an integral part of the grand interior decoration, the paintings were completely restored earlier this century. Although this may seem like a heavy-handed approach by today's standards, it aimed at aesthetic coherence, and as it currently poses no direct threat to the original paintings it will be left intact.

We know that many English wall paintings were covered over at some stage; and ours are no exception. The Dissolution of the Monasteries in 1536 saw the abandonment of monastic buildings, and the Civil War caused the obliteration of the religious images that decorated all types of ecclesiastical buildings. Castles were frequently abandoned as they were sacked, and often fell into a state of partial ruin. More modest wall paintings, such as those in domestic settings, while relatively unaffected by these events, did not entirely escape. Here fashion played its part. Once a wall painting became outdated, or simply dilapidated, it was usually covered, repainted, or panelled over. Worse damage came with the 19th century, when the fashion for bare stone walls led to the stripping away of historic plaster in many of the finest medieval buildings.

The idea that these wall paintings were historically important, and therefore to be safeguarded, came fairly late. The first public efforts at restoration came, ironically enough, with the failure of the 19th-century fresco revival at the Palace of Westminster. Almost immediately the artists were lambasted in the press for producing frescoes that were visibly deteriorating. Experiments to repair them were first made on Dyce's paintings in the Queen's Robing Room. A fixative coating, based on wax, was formulated by chemists, and when this failed, another more complex wax formula was prescribed, all to no avail. The paintings continued to deteriorate, and it would be many years before experts realised that wax was actually contributing to the damage.

Wax became the recommended treatment for all newly uncovered medieval paintings, and many of the wall paintings in our collection were waxed at this time. One of the earliest examples of the application of this so-called 'preservative' was the paintings at Kempley shortly after their uncovering in the 1870s. The methods used were fairly severe: at Westminster Abbey Chapter House, for instance, the paintings were sprayed with a jet of this fixative from a large pump, and the wax was then driven in with a blow-torch. Similar techniques were used at Farleigh Hungerford, as late as the 1930s.

The consequences of this treatment were universally disastrous: the wax effectively seals the painted surface, prevents the evaporation of moisture, and can darken with age. Remarkably, the use of wax remained widespread until 1953. Only then did an official committee recommend banning the use of wax in the conservation of wall paintings. This finally became official policy in 1959, in a report by the Council for the Care of Churches.

Much of the wall painting conservator's work over the last three decades has been to remove these wax coatings, often an enormous technical challenge. In many cases compromises have had to be made: at Longthorpe, for instance, the wax was painstakingly removed using a scalpel, but because the paint is so bound up with the wax, it could only be completely removed from unpainted areas, giving the images a false outlined effect. Recently, English Heritage has taken a step towards improving the situation by funding research into new treatment methods.

Surprisingly, the covering of paintings – by limewash, paint, or panel – has in many cases helped to preserve them. It is very likely that there are more wall paintings in English Heritage care still to be found. The dilemma for us now, if they are discovered, is whether it is really justified to reveal them and expose the paintings yet again to pollution, light, and other environmental perils.

The intimate link between a wall painting, the structure it is painted on, and its architectural context creates a unique set of problems. Wall paintings are always vulnerable to the immediate conditions of their environment. A simple problem such as a blocked drain or gutter, for instance, can cause enormous and irreparable damage. Or damage can occur more gradually over many years. Assessing the rate of damage is complex and can require collaboration between conservators, scientists, architects, and engineers. The multiplicity of factors involved can make it difficult to arrive at a single solution which suits the needs of the wall paintings and the historic building fabric as well as the people who may be using the buildings.

Although a policy of minimum intervention is ideal, wall paintings frequently require treatment, sometimes urgently. The practical treatment of wall paintings involves a range of activities including cleaning, plaster repairs, and paint consolidation. Methods have evolved quickly over the last decade, and techniques from a range of industries have been borrowed and adapted to wall painting conservation. For example, cleaning traditionally involved swabbing the dirt or coatings with a solvent, or mechanical removal with a tool such as a scalpel. Now methods have been developed so that cleaning materials may be applied in gel formulations or poultices, and a much wider range of tools is considered. Since no treatment to a wall painting is ever truly reversible, whatever is carried out must not affect the original, which can impose certain limitations on the conservator. The integrity of the painting is considered of paramount importance.

The conservation disasters of the last hundred years have been a sobering experience. The development of treatment methods is matched by our increasing ability to analyse and document the paintings, and this is vital if we want to hold on to our wall painting heritage. Generally speaking, the more we understand wall paintings, and the less we intervene, the better.

A conservator working on the wall paintings in the altar recess at Chester Castle

Belsay Castle

Finchale Priory

Richmond Castle

St Mary's Church, Studley Royal

Brodsworth Hall

Gainsborough Old Hall

Bolsover Little Castle

Chester Castle

Castle Acre Priory

Longthorpe Tower

Greyfriars

Stokesay Castle

Bushmead Priory

St Mary's Church, Kempley

Wrest Park

Blackfriars

Rycote Chapel

Hill Hall

Westminster Abbey

Chiswick House

Upnor Castle

Temple Manor

Farleigh Hungerford Castle

St Augustine's Abbey

Cleeve Abbey

Lullingstone Roman Villa

Dover Castle

Fiddleford Manor House

Portchester Castle

Hurst Castle

Osborne House

Berry Pomeroy Castle

English Heritage sites with known wall paintings

● These sites have individual entries in this book

(F) Denotes fragments in store

LONDON
● Chiswick House
● Westminster Abbey Chapter House

SOUTH EAST
Battle Abbey
Bayham Abbey
Bishops' Waltham Palace (F)
● Dover Castle
Fort Cumberland
● Hurst Castle
● Lullingstone Roman Villa
Netley Abbey
Old Soar Manor, Plaxtol
● Osborne House
Ospringe Manor House (F)
● Portchester Castle
Reculver Towers (F)
Richborough Roman Fort (F)
● Rycote Chapel
Silchester Roman City (F)
● St Augustine's Abbey, Canterbury
Titchfield Abbey
● Temple Manor, Strood
● Upnor Castle
Waverley Abbey

SOUTH WEST
● Berry Pomeroy Castle
● Blackfriars, Gloucester
● Cleeve Abbey
● Farleigh Hungerford Castle, St Leonard's Chapel
● Fiddleford Manor House
Hailes Abbey
Launceston Castle (F)
Muchelney Abbey
Okehampton Castle
St Briavel's Castle
● St Mary's Church, Kempley

EAST
● Bushmead Priory
● Castle Acre Priory
Castle Rising Castle
● Greyfriars, Great Yarmouth
● Hill Hall
● Longthorpe Tower
Tilbury Fort
● Wrest Park, Archer Pavilion

EAST MIDLANDS
● Bolsover Little Castle
● Gainsborough Old Hall

WEST MIDLANDS
Goodrich Castle
● Stokesay Castle
Wall Roman Site (F)
Wroxeter Roman City (F)

YORKSHIRE & THE HUMBER
Aldborough Roman Town (F)
● Brodsworth Hall
Byland Abbey
Easby Abbey
Kirkham Priory (F)
● Richmond Castle
Rievaulx Abbey (F)
Roche Abbey
● St Mary's Church, Studley Royal
St Peter's Church, Barton-on-Humber (F)
Wharram Percy

NORTH WEST
Baguley Hall (F)
● Chester Castle
Furness Abbey

NORTH EAST
● Belsay Castle
Brinkburn Priory
● Finchale Priory
Tynemouth Priory

St Mary's Church, Studley Royal

Using this book

The detailed and comprehensive guidebooks available for English Heritage properties give full information – historical, architectural, and anecdotal – about the properties in our care. This gazetteer of those sites which also contain wall paintings is intended to accompany and augment the guidebooks, giving detailed descriptions and historical information on the wall paintings, and allowing one to discover and explore these often overlooked treasures and gain a deeper insight into the history and life of these wonderful buildings.

This small volume is by no means comprehensive. Any attempt to compile a complete listing of wall paintings at English Heritage properties is complicated by the constant new discovery of painted areas, as well as by the acquisition of new sites. In addition, information revealed by our continuing research means that our 'collection' is never a static one, as we develop an ever increasing awareness of the paintings' history, significance, and social context.

For the purposes of this gazetteer it has been necessary to select only the highlights of our collection, strictly limiting our choices to paintings executed directly on to the building stone or plaster. Unfortunately this excludes other, often unique, examples of interior decoration, such as the painted steel girder in the Half Moon Battery at Pendennis Castle, and the Billiard Room mural, on wooden panels, at Eltham Palace. Other schemes of painting on inserted panels or on canvas glued directly to the wall can be seen at Audley End and Kenwood House.

In addition to the sites presented, we have also included a list of all our properties, region by region, which retain traces of painted decoration. These are important evidence of the previous existence of wall paintings, but their survival is now of purely academic interest. A reading list is also included for those who wish to know more about our wall paintings and the history of European wall painting practice in general.

Detail from Cupid and Psyche mural, Hill Hall

Chiswick House

The purpose of Chiswick House, the splendid Palladian villa designed by the Third Earl of Burlington (1694-1753), has always been unclear. Although a functioning house, it has been suggested that its role was more for conversation and entertainment, or perhaps to act as a private gallery, library, or club.

Whatever his intention, the Earl spared no expense on the design and fittings at Chiswick, and the splendid painted ceilings are proof of this. It is believed that William Kent designed the interiors and painted the ceilings, but this is not documented: there are no known payments to Kent in the Chiswick account books.

However, for stylistic reasons, the ceiling paintings are mainly attributed to Kent, as several of his pictorial trademarks are present here, such as finely painted grotesques and simulated mosaic backgrounds.

Kent, who had lived in Rome from 1709 to 1719, was a master of the Italianate style which was so attractive to Burlington and so appropriate for Chiswick. An example of this is in the Summer Parlour, thought to be the private drawing room of Lady Burlington, where Kent used panels of figurative scenes surrounded by intricate foliage, birds, and flowers.

Far right, portrait of William Kent in central ceiling panel, Red Velvet Room; right, the painted ceiling in the Red Velvet Room

The grander, ceremonial rooms were on the first floor, including the domed Saloon and two large painting galleries. Tucked away in the south corner, the Blue Velvet Room is one of the smallest rooms and yet some of the richest decoration was reserved for it. The room seems to have been intended for the entertainment of Burlington's acquaintances. Above luxurious blue silk-covered walls, the ceiling crowns the little chamber with its deep blue background, extensive gilding, and heavy, decorated cornice; the scheme's focus is on the large central scene, an allegory of Architecture.

In the Red Velvet Room the ceiling was designed as an accompaniment to some of Burlington's best pictures which hung on the walls underneath. It is painted with an allegory of the arts, clearly referring to the purpose of the room, and it is here that the ultimate clue to the authorship of the painting is found. The allegory for Painting is represented by a portrait of a man: none other than William Kent himself.

Left, detail of the Figure of Architecture in the Blue Velvet Room; below, the Blue Velvet Room; below left, one of the panels in the Summer Parlour

Westminster Abbey Chapter House

Completed in 1253, the Chapter House of Westminster Abbey has survived the vicissitudes of a chequered building history: from its primary role as the meeting place for the monks of the abbey, to becoming the temporary home of the first House of Commons between *c*1352 and 1395, and to being taken over for ecclesiastical councils until 1547, when it was finally converted into a record office. The building became empty in 1863 and was first restored by the architect Sir Giles Gilbert Scott between 1866 and 1872, and then again after bomb damage in 1941. Yet, despite these extensive restorations, certain exceptional aspects of the building's medieval history still survive, including unique 13th-century sculpture, a magnificent tiled pavement, and a series of remarkable wall paintings contained within the wall arcades.

Abbey records relate that these paintings were executed at the behest of John of Northampton, a monk of the abbey from 1372 to 1404. The scheme depicts, on the east wall arcade, the Last Judgement including the stunning depiction of Christ in Majesty, bordered by seraphim and cherubim. On the south-east wall, the first three bays contain a group of standing figures who look towards this eastern focus of the room. The rest of the painted bays contain scenes from the Apocalypse, including the life of St John the Divine. Along the base of the walls of the north-west and south-west bays, there are two schemes of painting: 15th-century animals, labelled in Gothic script, replace the original floral decoration. Originally comprising 96 individual scenes, the closest parallel to the Apocalypse scheme lies in a Bohemian panel painting displayed at the Victoria and Albert Museum.

There are three distinct painting styles at Westminster: the Last Judgement, with its softly modelled cherubim and an obvious use of the highest quality pigments and techniques, including *pastiglia* in the haloes (moulded plaster to create a relief effect); the large-scale figures in the south-east bay with their loose

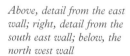

Above, detail from the east wall; right, detail from the south east wall; below, the north west wall

style and distinctive facial types; and the small-scale Apocalypse figures which are so close to contemporary Flemish and German painting. This does not necessarily mean that the paintings date from different periods; rather it is likely that they are by a number of different artists, and as such reflect the international artistic climate of the late 14th century. The technique of all the paintings is of the highest quality, as befits a cathedral in an important artistic centre, and includes glazing, gilding, and costly pigments such as indigo, vermilion, red lead, white lead, red lakes, and azurite.

At present the paintings are barely discernible beneath darkened layers of varnish and wax, the result of well-intentioned but inappropriate attempts at preservation earlier this century. It is therefore hoped that further research and scientific examination will determine whether it is feasible to improve their appearance by reducing these disfiguring coatings, allowing the visitor to appreciate these amazing and rare survivals of medieval art in London.

Dover Castle

As befits an important and strategic site which has seen continual use over the course of nine centuries, Dover Castle retains significant evidence of painted decoration. Yet because of this constant use, and although the type of decoration varies widely, the amount which survives is minimal.

We would expect to find in a medieval building of this calibre that many of the walls

were originally painted. The traditional form of medieval decoration, as in many sites in English Heritage care, is red line masonry pattern, meant to imitate fine ashlar walls. An example of this is the 13th-century red line masonry pattern on the north wall of the ground floor of the castle, in what is now the Regimental Museum.

In the Great Hall, a small fragment of the 14th-century painted foliate decoration survives on the west wall. Amazingly, although this is the tiniest of fragments, from it we can build a picture of what the room would have looked like in the 14th century. From documentary evidence we know that much of the castle was redecorated in 1329; and by comparing the style of the fragment with other known wall paintings, we see that it is very similar to other early 14th-century designs. It may have been part of a border used as an upper frieze to a large expanse of masonry pattern or perhaps to frame a series of large narrative scenes, as in an example at Burton Latimer (Northants).

The castle played a crucial defensive role during World Wars I and II and the building remained occupied by the army until 1956. The large late 19th-century Officer's Mess, situated on a prominent terrace at the southern end of the site, retains painted and drawn graffiti dating from around World War II. Most of the images consist of hand-drawn figures, faces, and text in pencil. Interestingly, one area retains a comprehensive listing of what appear to be paint colours and quantities, and the only signature, R Hanagan, dated 1963. In addition, a number of large figures and caricatures – including one of Winston Churchill – have been painted in bright colours with a dark black outline.

Above, detail of the early medieval decoration in the Great Hall; left, World War II graffiti

Hurst Castle

Hurst Castle was established in the 16th century to guard the western entrance to the Solent. Of chequered history, the castle itself was extensively remodelled during the 19th century.

The painting is located in a small room located in the west wing battery, which had been designated a theatre by soldiers who were stationed at the Castle during World War II. The wall painting appears to have been painted as a stage backdrop and covers the east face of a concrete traverse. It shows a kneeling male figure, hat held against his chest, who addresses a standing female figure in dress which would appear to be of the Stuart period. Perhaps this could refer to when Charles I was imprisoned at Hurst, as the castle is shown in the background. The proscenium arch, which surrounds the wall painting, is also painted with decorative motifs and the arms of the Royal Artillery.

The painting is clearly an amateur effort, and has been very simply executed using a very limited colour range in a stylised manner using blocks of colour, and perhaps a stencil. It is highly likely that the design was copied from a contemporary source such as a magazine. However, here the quality of the painting is irrelevant: it is a delightful insight into the daily lives of soldiers stationed at Hurst during World War II, and as such merits preservation.

The theatre stage situated in one of the west wing batteries

Lullingstone Roman Villa

Above, view into the Deep Room; below, detail of the painted niche

The Roman Villa at Lullingstone is believed to have been constructed *c*AD 75 and until the 4th century underwent constant architectural alteration. The building is essentially of the 'winged corridor type' comprising a rectangular range of rooms, fronted by an open verandah, which at either end opened out into large projecting rooms.

On the northern side the verandah leads directly into the cellar which dates to about AD 100, now called the 'Deep Room'. This room originally had two entrances, one of which was blocked by the insertion of a niche. Within this niche is a rare and important treasure: a painting of three female water deities or nymphs, of which only two figures survive. Reeds sprout from the hair of the central figure, who wears a delicate diadem, and blue water flows freely from her breasts. Perhaps the cellar had been used as a household shrine, relating to the well found within the room.

This painting is significant not only for its age – it is by far the earliest wall painting in English Heritage care – but also for the fact that it has survived *in situ*. This is very rare for excavated Roman wall paintings, especially in England.

Roman villas would originally have been painted throughout, and a large amount of painted plaster was discovered at Lullingstone during excavation. In particular, thousands of Early Christian wall painting fragments were found in the northern room. These have since been carefully pieced back together, and consist of two large 'Chi-Ro' monograms and six standing figures with their hands outstretched in prayer. Now held by the British Museum, and on display, these remains are important evidence of early Christian occupation and may represent the earliest Christian paintings in England.

Osborne House

William Dyce (1806-1864) was a proponent of fresco painting in England throughout his life, executing works in the medium at the new Houses of Parliament and the Buckingham Palace Garden Pavilion. When the Marine Residence at Osborne was built for Queen Victoria in 1845-6, Prince Albert, responsible for the design of much of the house, soon decided that the new staircase at Osborne should have a fresco. Because of his experience with the fresco medium, Dyce was commissioned to submit proposals for a large wall painting at the top of the main staircase. The painting took two months to complete, and is inscribed 'Aug 2 to Oct 7 1847'.

Dominating the Grand Staircase, just below the Nursery Landing, Neptune entrusting the Command of the Sea to Britannia was chosen for its fitting marine theme, and is an allegorical composition intended to suggest Britain's supremacy at sea. Neptune is shown relinquishing his trident and crown, symbols of his authority, in recognition of Britannia's right to rule over the sea.

Monumental painting, and true fresco painting in particular – whereby the painting is executed on wet plaster and the pigments are bound by a process of carbonation – enjoyed a brief revival throughout Europe during the second half of the 19th century. On the continent, this movement was led by a group of artists known as the Nazarenes, and Dyce was very closely associated with many of its members. In England, the revival centred on the decoration of the new Houses of Parliament, where, unfortunately, the paintings deteriorated quickly, which resulted in fresco soon going out of favour.

However, the painting at Osborne is an excellent example of William Dyce's aptitude as a painter, in a difficult medium and on such a large scale, and the good condition of the painting today is testimony to the durability of the true fresco medium when executed correctly and maintained in a suitable environment.

There are other examples of Prince Albert's interest in fresco painting throughout the house, for example the large framed painting of Hercules and Omphale by Gegenbaur (1830) in Prince Albert's Bathroom, and the collection of excavated Roman wall painting fragments.

Far right, 'Neptune entrusting the Command of the Sea to Britannia'; right, detail

Portchester Castle

The strategic location of Portsmouth Harbour secured the importance of Portchester Castle as a defensive base for many centuries; from its inception as a Roman fort in the 3rd century with its huge surrounding walls, there were numerous periods of building activity and the castle was ultimately used as a royal stronghold. Many highly important military campaigns set sail from Portchester, such as Henry V's departure for Agincourt in 1415. Although the significance of the castle declined after the Hundred Years War the building complex was finally used again as a prisoner-of-war camp during the Napoleonic Wars.

Given the imposing nature of the castle, it may seem strange that the original Norman keep is host to a large ornamental painting which survives, albeit severely damaged, on the second floor. This consists of two large decorative lozenges framed by swags in grand rococo style, between which is a roundel containing a depiction of the castle. Indeed, despite much research, why and when the scheme was painted has until recently proved mysterious.

It had always been thought that the scheme was perhaps painted by prisoners-of-war interned during the period 1794-1810 for use as a theatre backdrop, yet this conflicted with documentary evidence which located their theatre in the basement of the keep. In addition, recent technical examination has shown that the original colour range employed includes the blue pigment, French ultramarine, which was not available commercially in England until about 1830. Also, graffiti have been found etched within the area of painting dated 1840. These features, along with other structural changes found in the room, have now firmly placed the execution of the painting to the decade 1830-40.

As to why the scheme was painted, one piece of evidence may provide the answer: the castle was privately owned during the 19th century but records refer to a Mr Sutton who was permitted to use a room in the keep to stage plays and 'who has left as a record, some mural paintings there'. It is therefore logical to speculate that the castle tradition of theatrical performances was continued by the local population long after the military left Portchester in 1819.

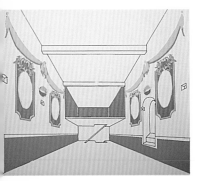

Above, reconstruction drawing of how the room would have looked in the 19th century; right, the north wall; far right, roundel illustrating Portchester Castle

Rycote Chapel

This small chapel, dedicated to St Michael and All Angels and built on the site of a former Benedictine chapel, once served the great house at Rycote. Constructed in 1449, it appears from the exterior to be a high-quality example of Perpendicular architecture; however, it is the 17th-century fittings inside the chapel that make it exceptional.

Sir John Williams, who bought Rycote in the 16th century, was a figure of considerable importance at court and guardian to Princess Elizabeth. The two family pews in the chapel were erected by the Williams family, one of them for the exclusive use of Princess Elizabeth; when the estate passed to the Norreys family, Elizabeth, now the Queen, remained a frequent visitor. It was Francis Norreys (owner from 1603 to 1622) who was responsible for the further decoration of the chapel, including the addition of painting, and the building of a western gallery and a musicians' gallery over the north pew.

Chapter records from 27 January 1612 note that 'the whole space between the Organs and the pillars over the knightes stalls should be colored blue, & be sett with starres guilded.' This probably refers to the ceilings of the Western Gallery and the Norreys Pew, which are painted with stylised representations of the heavens, with clouds (their edges accented in red and blue) in a blue sky studded with applied gilded stars. The wagon roof is painted in imitation marbling with the same gold stars decorating the laths.

Detailed examination of the stars, interestingly enough, has provided the critical clue in forming a secure date for the paintings. By looking at the reverse, one can see that they are made from 17th-century French playing cards. Furthermore, the cards are likely to be from before 1628, when Charles I forbade any further imports of continental playing cards and the London company of makers of playing cards was founded. The discovery of this novel way of reusing cards that were no longer in fashion has been extremely useful in ascribing the paintings with some confidence to the second decade of the 17th century.

Above left, the Norreys Pew; below left, detail; below, one of the star-shaped cutouts

St Augustine's Abbey, Canterbury

The abbey was founded in 598 by St Augustine himself and is therefore one of the oldest and most important monastic sites in the country.

After the Norman Conquest, a nominee of King William dismantled the east end of the Saxon church and built a new crypt, now known as the 'Norman Crypt'. In 1325 the crypt altar was rededicated to St Mary and the Angels Michael, Gabriel, and Raphael, at which time it has also been suggested that the rounded chapel was squared-off and the wall plaster painted.

The surviving decoration probably relates to this period, and what survives can be found on the north wall of the chapel. It consists of an interlaced medallion pattern in red and yellow, with foliate decoration within the resulting lozenges. This painting is extremely important evidence of the early appearance of the crypt chapel. Although somewhat sheltered, it is truly remarkable that in a ruined site it survives *in situ*, a testimony to the strength and durability of medieval paintings.

Further evidence of the early decoration of the cathedral has been found in the form of excavated wall plaster fragments, some of them of extremely high quality. These originate mainly from St Thomas's Chapel (13th century) and show the use of expensive materials such as gold leaf.

Above, view into the Norman crypt; below, detail of the painting

Temple Manor

It is hard to imagine that this 13th-century manor house, now marooned in the middle of an industrial estate on the west bank of the river Medway and standing in only half an acre of land, once used to provide lodgings for the Knights Templar, the military religious order established during the Crusades in the Holy Land to defend the Holy Sepulchre and Christian pilgrims. All that survives is a stone building with a 17th-century brick extension at either end, but originally the site contained a complex of timber structures to which the present detached building was added c1240.

The building contains a first-floor hall, reached by an external staircase, which was originally divided into an outer chamber, thought to have served as a public room for conducting business, and an inner chamber which provided privacy for visiting dignitaries. The north and south walls of the outer chamber have wall arcades with arches rising from continuous seats (three on the north and five on the south), originally with Purbeck marble shafts.

As befits the ascetic ideals of an Order living under stern monastic discipline, the wall plaster throughout is decorated with masonry pattern in red on a white background, with various simple decorative motifs in black and yellow. Although fragmentary, these remains provide a fascinating glimpse of the original appearance of the room and the type of decoration familiar to a member of the Knights Templar. This is in stark contrast to the decidedly urban setting in which we find Temple Manor today.

Left, view of the hall; above, detail of painted masonry pattern

Upnor Castle

The castle at Upnor is a rare example of an Elizabethan gun-fort. Built in 1559 to protect Elizabeth I's warships moored near the new dockyards at Chatham, the building was designed by Sir Richard Lee and further altered between 1599 and 1601 when a defensive ditch, timber palisade, drawbridge, and gatehouse where constructed. Over the following century the castle's strategic importance declined and the building was eventually converted for use as a magazine for munitions.

A surprising and exciting discovery was made in 1941 as a result of damage incurred by bombing during World War II. The force of the explosion disturbed internal plaster within the South Tower of the Gate House, and on the second floor a fascinating drawing of a ship was revealed. The painting was examined (and possibly fully uncovered and treated) in April 1949 by Charles Mitchell of the Warburg Institute and Michael Robinson of the National Maritime Museum, who describe the decoration as follows:

Above, painted decoration in the guardroom; right, the ship painting in the clock room

`There is a quite clear spritsail topmast which could not appear in big ships after 1720. The curved shape of the head would pass for anything after 1660. There is one obscurity. The figurehead has the appearance of the fiddle head type which means a date about 1800. In the late 17th or early 18th century there would have been a lion figurehead, but this is a crude drawing and what looks like a fiddle head is very probably shorthand for a lion figurehead. There is one other explanation, namely, that this is a consciously archaic but inaccurate drawing of an older ship drawn by a man who lived in the days of the fiddle head, but that is a remote and unlikely possibility. The spritsail topmast would have passed from the memory of most practical seamen by 1800. We incline to date the drawing about 1700.'

Traces of possibly earlier decoration also exist in an adjacent guardroom, composed of black bands and a stencilled strapwork pattern, and it is highly likely that further painting awaits discovery in other areas of the building.

Blackfriars, Gloucester

The priory at Blackfriars, in central Gloucester, was first mentioned in 1241 when a royal grant of 20 marks was made towards the building. By 1265 it was recorded as more or less complete, with considerable enlargements in the late 13th and mid 14th centuries. After the Dissolution, the house was purchased by Thomas Bell, who converted the church into a residence for himself, and the priory into a factory. It was maintained as a domestic and commercial property until it came into the care of English Heritage.

There is evidence of painted decoration throughout the priory, including traces of paint within the carrels in the library, remains of an inscription on the recently-exposed lavabo, and paint which may relate to Bell's later conversion of the church building. However, by far the most important survival is the 16th-century painting within the window splays in the east range, once the Abbot's Lodgings.

The decoration was once remarkably complex, consisting of foliage, birds, and rosettes against a reddish-brown background, with traces of a patron figure and scrolls bearing inscriptions. The scheme is likely to have been used throughout the ground floor of the east range and clearly originally extended beyond the existing east wall. Painted imitation tapestry was popular throughout the Middle Ages, in both ecclesiastical and secular settings, and there are several examples within English Heritage's collection alone, such as at Gainsborough Old Hall and Belsay Castle. Stylistically, a close comparison can be made between Blackfriars and the painted imitation tapestry in the Ballroom at Bramall Hall, Cheshire (*c*1500).

Unfortunately, in the 30 years since their discovery the paintings have deteriorated rapidly and are now in an extremely damaged, although stable, condition. Photographs taken in the 1960s show the remarkably high quality of the paintings, but sadly, these pictures all too clearly emphasise the fragile nature of medieval decoration.

Above, the nave of the church with traces of post-medieval paint over the fireplace; left, reconstruction of the painting in the window splay of the Abbot's Lodgings; below, the painting in the Abbot's Lodgings today

Berry Pomeroy Castle

The wall painting in the gatehouse at Berry Pomeroy Castle is one of the most remarkable English wall painting discoveries of recent years, and as such is one of the most important paintings in the guardianship of English Heritage. Its discovery was fascinating: in 1978 a chargehand at the castle caught a glimpse of a face under a thick growth of moss and ivy. Specialists were quickly called in to uncover the painting, which turned out to be an exceptionally elaborate late medieval Adoration of the Magi.

Substantial remains of contemporary red paint survive throughout the first floor of the gatehouse, but the Adoration, located above the window on the east wall of the east tower, appears to have been the only figure subject within the room and is important evidence that this part of the chamber was used as a chapel or oratory. It is a complex representation of the Adoration, with the holy family shown in the stable, a shepherd and other onlookers witnessing the scene, and a distant landscape of hills, trees, and buildings.

In both composition and details the painting shows strong Netherlandish influence, typical of high-quality paintings of the late 15th and early 16th centuries, while the costume suggests a date of *c*1490-1500. It has been compared to the celebrated scheme in Eton College Chapel (1479-87) and the wall paintings of similar date at Durham Deanery, but the most striking parallel can be found in the wall painting of the same subject in the chancel of St Mary de Crypt, Gloucester. Also in common with the wall painting at Gloucester is the inclusion of a black king, a feature which became popular in German art in the second half of the 15th century and spread to the rest of Europe by 1510, making this one of the earliest examples in England of this pictorial type.

Typical of Netherlandish-influenced wall paintings, the Adoration is quite sophisticated technically, as confirmed by recent technical analysis. The colour range includes vermilion, red lead, and copper green, all pigments that are incompatible with lime. This means that the painting was not executed in the true fresco technique (painted without a binder into fresh lime plaster), but that the pigments must have been applied in an organic medium such as oil. The potential fragility of such a technique makes it all the more remarkable that this painting survives today.

Far right, the east wall of the gatehouse; below, detail of the Adoration

Cleeve Abbey

The survival of any decorative painting in a Cistercian context is rare, especially in England. Because of the Cistercian Order's conservative views on art, widely known through the writings of St Bernard of Clairvaux and others, it may seem surprising that any decorative work at all was undertaken by this order. But for the student of medieval art, the development of decorative work at Cistercian sites is a fascinating way to witness their gradual increase in tolerance of decoration. A fine example is the 13th-century Cistercian abbey at Cleeve, Somerset, which retains highly important remains of wall painting throughout its claustral buildings.

The Sacristy is a small barrel-vaulted room which retains an important tiled floor and extensive remains of painted decoration throughout the walls and vault. This includes single red line masonry pattern, a wavy-line frieze, and a chevron pattern, as well as an elaborate foliage border which bisects the vault. In particular, the piscina – a small niche with a sink in its base meant for the cleansing of liturgical vessels – retains a significant amount of painting, including unusual stylised floral sprays and rosettes. Masonry pattern survives in other areas of the east range including the Library, Dorter, Parlour, and Common Room. The Chapter House contains extensive areas of original plaster decorated with masonry pattern on the vaults, the borders of which are decorated with looped scrollwork containing wide-spaced chevron pattern.

Above, old photograph of the Frater showing traces of a crucifixion on the east wall; right, the Painted Chamber

The south range boasts the remarkable Frater, or refectory, and a small room known as the Painted Chamber. The location of the Painted Chamber, directly off the main staircase and next to the dining area, indicates that it held some importance in the administration of the abbey, and its elaborate decoration certainly supports this. The decoration consists of an imitation tapestry scheme which survives on the east and west walls and within the south window splay. It is mainly decorative in nature, except for the east wall which contains a large figurative scene, which can easily be described as the most important late Cistercian wall painting in Britain. In the centre an old man is depicted standing on a bridge between a lion and a dragon, while above his head are two angels apparently bearing the symbols of the Passion. To the left stands St Margaret driving her lance into the mouth of a small dragon at her feet. For many years the precise subject matter was unclear, and it has only recently been reidentified by Miriam Gill (Courtauld Institute) as a legend from the late medieval Gesta Romanorum. There are remains of painting in several other areas of the south range, including graffiti within the corridor outside the Painted Chamber, the room above the Painted Chamber, and the ground floor (Corrodians' Lodgings).

After the Dissolution much of Cleeve was destroyed and the abbey eventually became a working farm. It is incredible to think of cows inhabiting the Sacristy, and even more amazing that, in spite of this, any decoration survived. There were some casualties, however. Documentary evidence records the presence of a Crucifixion with the Virgin and St John on the east wall of the refectory which would have been extremely rare. However, tests have shown that this scheme was lost – largely destroyed – at some stage.

Above, the Chapter House, looking west; left, the piscina in the Sacristy with detail below

Farleigh Hungerford Castle

Above, 19th-century watercolour of St Anne's Chapel, showing the interior fully painted; right, the nave east wall, St Leonard's Chapel

St Leonard's Chapel, within the ruinous castle walls at Farleigh Hungerford, is significant both for its monuments and extensive remains of wall paintings. When one enters the church, the interior is somewhat confusing: what you see is a palimpsest of decorative schemes, many of them overlapping each other, that range in date from the 15th to the 19th century.

The earliest decoration appears to be that commissioned by Sir Walter Hungerford in the 15th century, which includes a grey and white brocade pattern and is dominated by the large St George in the south-east corner. St George, the patron saint of soldiers and the kingdom of England, grew extremely popular during the Crusades of the 12th century. Although this made him a frequent subject in English medieval wall painting, he was rarely shown standing, and this painting is one of only four known examples in this country. Next to St George, just barely visible on the south wall, was a portrait of a knight in shining silver chain mail and rich armour embellished with gold, also against a grey and white brocade background. Recent analysis of the pigments has shown that these paintings were originally of the highest possible quality, painted with rare and expensive pigments such as vermilion, orpiment, verdigris, and lead tin yellow, as well as gold and silver leaf.

A distinct scheme of painting is found in the small side chapel, called St Anne's. In 1648, Margaret, the wife of Edward Hungerford, commissioned the decoration of the chapel in honour of her husband. Their white marble tomb, of exceptional quality, can be found in the centre of the chapel. Remains of the paintings are visible on the ceiling beams and the east corner of the north wall, but the original appearance of the room – a complete decorative ensemble covering all four walls and the ceiling – can be gleaned from early watercolours of the interior. The survival of any wall painting from the mid 17th century – a period of known political instability – especially in a religious context is rare in England, making even these scant remains in St Anne's Chapel extremely important.

Further traces of possibly 17th-century painting have been found in the nave, and in the 18th century it seems that the large coat-of-arms on the east wall and possibly the corresponding lozenges on the east and west walls were executed. In the 19th century, by which time the chapel windows had been blocked, a theatre painter from Bath carried out a scheme of architectural motifs of which only faint traces remain on the east wall. The decoration found at Farleigh is a fine example of the way in which wall paintings can demonstrate changing attitudes and tastes over the course of several hundred years.

St George

St Mary's Church, Kempley

St Mary's, Kempley is a good example of the type of small medieval parish church that still exists in large numbers in remote parts of England. However, this church is significant in that it contains several schemes of wall paintings which are truly exceptional for their extent and quality.

Kempley is best known for its impressive scheme of Romanesque wall painting, one of the most important in England. The majority of the 12th-century scheme (generally dated to about 1130/40) is restricted to the chancel and the east wall of the nave (the chancel arch). The scheme was rediscovered in 1871 by the local vicar, and further conserved from the 1950s to the 1970s.

The paintings in the chancel form an Apocalypse scheme. This includes, on the barrel vault, a Christ in Majesty surrounded by the four evangelists, four archangels, the sun, the moon, and stars. On the north and south walls, seated apostles look upwards toward the vault. Standing bishops and pilgrims complete the scheme at the east end. Several aspects of the iconography point to foreign sources, and in fact are thought to refer directly to the pilgrimage to Santiago de Compostela. Figures of pilgrims, in painted niches on the north and south wall of the chancel, have been the subject of much conjecture: one may be the figure of St James the Greater, but the others remain unidentified.

In the nave, over the chancel arch, an interesting depiction of the Three Maries at the Sepulchre can be seen on the south side, flanking a chevron pattern which once formed the backdrop for a sculptured rood (crucifix). This subject is extremely rare and was only recently identified when a 17th-century beam was removed from across the top of the painting. It shows three female figures holding a large cloth – meant to represent a temporary

Below, the north wall of the nave; below right, wall painting on the underside of the chancel arch

Easter Sepulchre, once commonly used in medieval liturgical drama. The closest parallel to this is found in the wall paintings of St-Sernin, Toulouse. The 12th-century decoration continued along the uppermost portion of the north and south walls; however, owing to later replastering and overpainting in the 15th century, the subject-matter here remains a mystery.

The paintings in the nave have only been clarified more recently, as they comprise several, often overlapping, schemes dating from the 14th, 15th, and 17th centuries. On the north wall, for example, there is a Wheel of Life, and figures of St Anthony with St Michael and the Virgin, as well as large areas of masonry pattern. A large figure of St Christopher, partially obliterated by a window, is at the west end of the north wall. On the south wall, there are several different phases of painting, including a Martyrdom of St Thomas à Becket, a possible St Margaret, and other subjects, all providing a dense and remarkable overview of medieval painting types.

The vault of the chancel

Fiddleford Manor

The stunning 14th-century oak roofs in the hall and solar of Fiddleford Manor inspired Pevsner to describe this medieval interior as the most spectacular in Dorset. However, the recent discovery of a splendid contemporary painting of the Annunciation has enhanced this room even further.

The painting, located on the north wall of the solar on either side of the window, was discovered beneath layers of limewash in 1990 as part of a general conservation programme. Until then, the only clues that there might be some original decoration were the small traces of red paint visible to the east of the window where overlying limewash had flaked away. An Annunciation scene was revealed with on the west side an angel holding a scroll with the inscription Ave Maria Gracia Plena, clearly a depiction of the Angel Gabriel. There would have been a figure of the Virgin on the east side, facing Gabriel, but unfortunately, apart from the bottom corner of her robe, the Virgin had been lost as a result of earlier plaster repairs, and even Gabriel suffers from extensive damage and loss. The scheme has been dated to the last quarter of the 14th century.

An Annunciation scene may seem inappropriate for a domestic interior, but religious subject-matter was commonly used in secular medieval wall paintings. Contemporary parallels can be seen in Longthorpe Tower (Cambs), also in English Heritage care. The arrangement of the Annunciation on either side of an opening is also reasonably typical and is found in the14th-century scheme at Prior Crauden's Chapel, Ely, and as far afield as Giotto's Arena Chapel, Padua.

Right, the archangel Gabriel

Bushmead Priory

All that survives of Bushmead Priory, a typical small Augustinian priory founded *c*1195, is the impressive refectory building. Traditionally, refectories were found on the south side of the cloister, but at Bushmead it was built on the north side so that the kitchens would have direct access to the river.

The original decoration of the refectory is not known, but the present scheme seems to have been executed around 1310. The main element of the decoration is masonry pattern, here consisting of single red horizontal lines, and double red vertical lines. The second vertical line is thinner, giving a certain illusion of depth to the design. In the centre of each 'block' of masonry is a deep red five-lobed rosette, probably executed using a stencil, with a white centre. The masonry pattern covers only the upper walls, continuing to a height 2 metres above the floor, where it terminates in a thick red band. The lower walls were unpainted, and may have originally been covered with wainscoting or textile hangings.

Fascinating details can be discovered higher up in the building. The uppermost frieze, which runs along the gable rafters of the east and west walls, consists of naturalistic vines with small flowers. On the west wall, on the south side, the vine-pattern frieze emerges from the beak of a crane-like bird, and on the north side it terminates in a figure of a hooded man. Within and around the west window the decoration includes geometric patterns and imitation marble columns.

On the north wall, running along the wall-plate, is a series of diamond-shaped frames containing small figurative scenes, bordered by a wave pattern. If we look at the westernmost edge, we can see a scene which has recently been interpreted as the Creation of Eve. The figure of Eve is shown emerging from a reclining Adam; she faces towards the right and has both arms raised, held by the wrists by God, whose left hand is raised in blessing. The paintings are extremely refined and have been compared to the tiny details – called *marginalia* – found in manuscript illuminations. In style, they have been compared to the highly-sophisticated wall paintings at Sigena, in northern Spain, and Easby church, North Yorkshire.

Far left, detail of the Creation of Eve; centre and right, details of decorative patterns in the refectory

Hill Hall

The splendid early Elizabethan manor house at Hill Hall, Essex, contains one of the gems of the English Heritage wall painting collection. The building alone is significant for many reasons: built by the courtier and diplomat Sir Thomas Smith, it is of considerable architectural interest. However, it is the wall paintings within that make Hill Hall even more special. They are a unique example of high-quality figurative wall painting from a period – at least in England – where very little of this calibre survives.

That the paintings survive at all is nothing short of remarkable. The building was altered considerably over the course of three centuries, and from 1947 to 1952 Hill Hall was used – unlikely as it may seem – as a prison. In 1969, a fire ravaged much of the building, damaging the paintings even further.

Today, large areas of painting only survive in two rooms, but fragments found throughout the house show that, amazingly, almost all of the rooms would have been painted in a similar way. There appear to be two distinct cycles of painting: the Old Testament story of King Hezekiah, and the story of Cupid and Psyche, based on Lucius Apuleius' *Metamorphoses*. The Cupid and Psyche series is painted as a series of imitation tapestries, indicated by the thick borders richly painted with fruit and leaves which imitate Brussels tapestry work. It very closely follows a series of Italian engravings, with only minor changes to the composition. The Hezekiah series, on the other hand, although based on 16th-century woodcuts by the Flemish artist Bernard Salomon, is a looser interpretation of the engraving, and far more

Detail from the Cupid and Psyche cycle

sophisticated in style than the Cupid and Psyche paintings. This unusual mixture of biblical and classical themes has led to the suggestion that they were specifically chosen by Smith – a great scholar and aesthete – for personal reasons. Several books known to be in his library suggest that he had an interest not only in the arts generally but in the specific themes used in these paintings, and it is entirely possible that he worked closely with the painter in their design.

The identity of the painter, however, is still a mystery. The strong continental influences have led some to suggest that the artist was not English; the name of Lucas de Heere, a Flemish painter known to be in England at this time, has even been put forward. However, there is no reason to believe that English artists were not working in this style, and to this exceptional standard, during the 16th century.

Details from the Hezekiah cycle

Castle Acre Priory

Above, details of the 13th-century scheme; right, the Prior's Chapel; far right, detail from the east wall

In many cases, the gradual deterioration of medieval wall paintings over the course of several centuries, coupled with the changing use of a building, results in them being forgotten, and it is only with determined research that they are rediscovered. As the paintings become more faint the records become more sparse. A good example of this is the prior's chapel at Castle Acre Priory.

The Cluniac priory of Castle Acre is believed to have been founded around 1090 by William de Warenne, second Earl of Surrey. The wall paintings are found in the prior's private chapel in the Prior's Lodgings, which is on the first floor within the western range of buildings, originally constructed in the early 12th century.

Two records from the 1950s had noted the survival of wall paintings in the chapel. One of these described a figure of a bishop or abbot and various coats-of-arms, and another mentioned traces of gold stars and crowns.

However, today, the fragmentary nature of the wall paintings means that they are extremely difficult to see, and they were assumed to be largely lost.

It was only recently, during investigations by English Heritage, that these paintings were rediscovered. Armed with the documentary evidence and trained eyes, conservators found through very close examination that there were three main phases of painting surviving in the chapel. These ranged from rare 12th-century Romanesque paintings to schemes from the 15th century. One area in particular, which appears to date to the late 13th century, includes a crowned figure under a canopy, tentatively identified as a Virgin and Child. This was painted with extreme delicacy and was of the highest possible quality.

The rediscovery of the paintings at Castle Acre shows how valuable it can be to carry out full documentary research of wall painting sites in conjunction with on-site examination

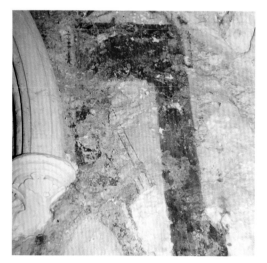

Greyfriars, Great Yarmouth

.That any wall paintings have survived at Greyfriars Cloisters, Great Yarmouth, is a miracle. The original 13th-century friary managed to escape the destruction of the Dissolution, only to be later demolished and reused over the course of 400 years until the church and many of the buildings had all but disappeared and become encased within more modern buildings. It was only after World War II bomb damage that two tomb recesses were discovered. These would have been located on the south wall of the south transept of the original church. They can now be viewed from a small wooden platform, entered from an opening in the lower part of the wall.

The painting survives on the back wall of the west tomb recess and shows a figurative scene with a female figure positioned within an elaborate architectural framework which has been dated to c1300. It is possible that the female figure represents the Virgin, and that traces of another figure, turning towards her in prayer, may be a donor portrait. Both tombs are surrounded by finely sculpted canopies which retain extensive fragments of red and greenish-blue paint, although part of the west canopy has been destroyed by the insertion of a later fireplace. The undersides of the arches of both tombs contain the remains of a geometric diamond pattern, again executed in red and blue, with a central circular motif. The style is extremely sophisticated, and the remains of high-quality pigments, such as the microscopic remains of gold leaf in certain areas, provide a sense of the superb quality of these paintings.

The painting at Greyfriars has been compared to a wall painting at Little Wenham church in Suffolk. This painting, dated to c1310-20, contains three female saints positioned within a very similar architectural setting. Both paintings also exhibit the same fine lines and delicate execution as well as extensive remains of a green/blue pigment, most likely verdigris, a popular pigment in use during this period, particularly in East Anglia.

Above, detail of female figure; left, the canopy itself retains traces of paint; below left, detail of painted architectural canopy

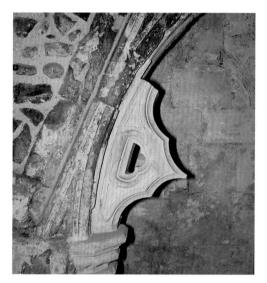

Within the tiny unimposing tower at Longthorpe is found one of the most complete and important schemes of medieval secular painting of its date in Europe. The tower, built *c*1300, forms part of an earlier fortified manor house owned by the de Thorpe family, and the decoration may have been commissioned by Robert de Thorpe, steward of Peterborough Abbey until 1329, or his son, also named Robert, who was appointed steward in 1330 and still held Thorpe in 1346.

The paintings, which survive virtually intact, cover both the walls and vault of the Great Chamber on the first floor of the tower. They were rediscovered in 1945, when the tenant of the adjoining house began renovations to the tower after its occupation by the Home Guard during World War II.

The extraordinarily varied subject matter comprises a rich combination of religious, didactic, and secular subjects. Once described as a 'spiritual encyclopedia', it includes several extremely rare subjects such as a Wheel of the Senses, with the senses represented symbolically around the rim of the wheel: Taste as a monkey eating, Touch as a spider's web, Smell as a vulture, Hearing as a boar, and Sight as a cockerel. In wall painting, the only other surviving example of this subject in wheel format dates from the 13th century, in the Cistercian Abbey of Tre Fontane near Rome.

There are popular images, such as the Twelve Labours of the Months, and the Seven Ages of Man – including the Infant in its cradle, the Boy with a ball and whip, Youth, Manhood with a hawk and lure, Middle Age, Old Age carrying a bag full of savings, and Decrepitude on crutches – each of them labelled in Lombardic script. There are also several images which refer to everyday life at Longthorpe, such as the depiction of a basket-maker, a common sight in this fenland area, and a bestiary which includes several types of local birds.

Paradoxically, the complexity of the scheme at Longthorpe belies what is really a rather ordinary manorial context and this suggests that such paintings, probably based on contemporary literary sources, were more widespread than we realise.

The Nativity

The Wheel of the Senses

Wrest Park, Archer Pavilion

The Archer Pavilion, which lies to the south of the mansion of Wrest Park, at the base of the Long Water, consists of a small domed rotunda with radiating square- and round-ended chambers. It was designed by Thomas Archer, and was built as a picturesque retreat in the baroque style for the residents of the Park. It could have been used for activities such as taking tea, but was also equipped for more extended stays with bedrooms, a kitchen, and a privy.

One is immediately struck by the sharp contrast between the simple exterior and the rich and detailed decoration inside. The interior and the porch are entirely painted with trompe l'oeil work that conceals several doors which open into small passages. These would have been for the servants' use and lead into the kitchens in the basement and the servants'

Below, the domed ceiling; below right, the porch

quarters upstairs. The dome is painted with a imitation coffered ceiling, and the base of the dome is painted with feigned architecture incorporating busts in niches and figures flanking coats of arms and urns.

The painting is signed and dated `Hauduroy pinxit 1712', and is one of two known works to survive in England by Louis Hauduroy, a French painter who was active *c*1700. His other scheme, at Culverthorpe Hall in Lincolnshire, has only recently been rediscovered. Although the paintings in the Archer Pavilion have been heavily restored, they are still a rare example of the baroque style in England and as such form an important part of the English Heritage collection.

Gainsborough Old Hall

Gainsborough Old Hall is a large timber-framed medieval manor house with late 16th- and early 17th-century additions, and is remarkable for its almost complete survival to the present day. The east range originally comprised two floors and housed the main ceremonial rooms, including the Lower Great Chamber.

This room contains significant remains of decorative wall painting, mainly on the west wall. It is painted directly on the stud-and-plaster – a typical late-medieval construction of timbers with plaster beds between them – and has been tentatively dated to the late 16th century. However, this type of domestic decoration was so common throughout the 16th and 17th centuries that it is difficult to date with any precision.

The wall painting at Gainsborough was intended to mask the wall with an imitation of tapestry hangings, and along the top of the painting the painted nails, loops, and swags are just discernible. As befits a house of this calibre, the painting is quite sophisticated in terms of style and technique, and includes foliage, swags, bells, birds, inscriptions, and draw-string flagons. The remains of a peacock tail are also visible, as well as areas of Gothic-style lettering. All of these elements were combined to imitate the rich tapestries which no doubt adorned the upper, more important chambers of the Old Hall.

Left, the remains of decorative wall painting; above, detail

Bolsover, Little Castle

The Hall

The Hall, one of the Labours of Hercules

Above, the Ante-Room, one of the Four Temperaments; right, the Elysium Room

Designed as a romantic version of a medieval keep by the architect Robert Smythson for Sir Charles Cavendish, and his heir William, the Little Castle encapsulates every element of the late Renaissance fascination with allegory and myth, intended to delight and mystify like an episode from *The Faerie Queene*. The wall paintings are part of this conception, and rely on a theatrical yet complex iconography entirely in keeping with a building used to hosting lavish court masques and pageants. All the painted schemes throughout the building (in addition to wall paintings the castle contains painted panels and architectural decoration) were completed during Sir William's time, although – to add to the general air of mystery surrounding the building – none of the original artists is known.

The wall paintings in the Ante-room, to the left of the entrance porch, are situated in lunettes above the panelling and depict The Four Elements and The Four Temperaments. Each individual scene has been copied from a set of prints by Pieter Jode (1570–1634), after Martin de Vos (1531–1603) where three of the temperaments are shown figuratively: the phlegmatic, the melancholic, and the choleric, with the exception of the sanguine. For example, a fisherman and his wife express the cold and damp nature of their temperament.

In the adjacent Hall, the paintings depict scenes from the labours of Hercules, who was assigned twelve tasks to complete in penance for killing his wife and children. The paintings show the figure of Hercules in combat with animals he was obliged to subdue, although only four labours are shown: the Nemean Lion, Diomedes Mares, the Cretan Bull, and the Wild Boar of Erymanthus. The scenes may have been selected to symbolise Man

overcoming his animal passions. In addition, panels to either side of the chimney breast on the north wall show Hercules and Vulcan the god of fire. The paintings may have been based on engravings by an Italian painter and engraver, Antonio Tempesta.

On the first floor, the painted scheme in the Elysium room shows an assembly of pagan gods. On the main ceiling, the composition of which is thought to have been derived from an engraving by Cornelius Cort of a ceiling by Primaticcio in the Galerie l'Ulysse at Fontainbleu, various deities are set against a *trompe l'oeil* sky. The painting continues on a frieze at the top of the walls and shows, among others, Juno and Minerva, while the window arch contains a figure of Neptune with a scroll inscribed 'All is vanite'. On the underside of the arch are the figures of Democritus laughing and Heraclitus weeping.

In contrast to the pagan themes of the Elysium room the painted ceiling in the Heaven room illustrates Christ ascending into Heaven. In the corners of the room cherubs hold music sheets of 'Three country dances in one' composed by Thomas Ravenscroft *c*1609 and within the frieze angels display symbols of the Passion.

Stokesay Castle

Stokesay Castle is certainly one of the finest surviving manor houses in England. Its importance lies in its largely unaltered state, as an example of a compact, defensible, domestic unit. Despite its militaristic appearance Stokesay was very much a home, and there was a clear emphasis on comfort. Indeed, contemporary records indicate that there was glazing in the residential areas – an early example of such luxury in a manorial context.

The hall and solar block are known to have been built by Laurence de Ludlow, a wealthy wool merchant, in the last quarter of the 13th century. The north tower belongs to an earlier phase of building, thought to be *c*1200. It was begun as a stone solar tower, probably associated with a timber hall, and its basement was clearly a pantry and buttery area. It still retains its original beaten earth floor, as well as a rectangular pit in its northern projection, which probably served as an ice store.

Painted decoration survives on the upper parts of the north-west, north, and west walls of the room, with fragmentary remains on the others. It consists of scrollwork design in red, and presumably would have originally covered the entire wall surface. The freehand appearance of the scrollwork suggests that it is from the second quarter of the 14th century, but such designs can be difficult to date with any precision as there are no firmly dated examples. These designs were meant to evoke the sort of tapestry hangings that would have been found in some of the other, more formal rooms of the castle.

The context of the paintings is rather curious: as the basement room was clearly a service area, why would it have been painted? It seems that at some stage the room's function must have changed, perhaps to a parlour or bedchamber. However, there is no evidence of a fireplace or hearth in the room. The circumstances of these paintings therefore remain a mystery.

There are other, more fragmentary, remains of decorative painting throughout the rest of the castle. These include traces in the Great Hall and a significant amount of late medieval painting within the garderobe. The garderobe is indeed an unusual location for painted decoration, and here it includes flowers and stars, perhaps part of an imitation *millefleurs* tapestry, which would indeed have been the height of luxury.

Right, detail from the Buttery; far right, view of the Buttery interior

Brodsworth Hall

Charles Sabine Augustus Thellusson (1822–1850) commissioned Brodsworth Hall after inheriting the estate of his great-grandfather, Peter Thellusson, in 1859. He demolished the earlier Georgian mansion and began building the present house in 1861, completing it by 1870. The new hall was constructed according to the design of Chevalier Casentini, an Italian architect and sculptor.

Much of the interior of the house is decorated with sombre painted marbling, but the Drawing Room is more elegant and delicate in style. The ceiling, coving, and cornice of the Drawing Room are painted with arabesque ornamentation, bird motifs, and garlands of flowers, in vivid pinks and greens with extensive gilding. There is no mention in the 1861 specification of this decorative scheme. Instead it describes satinwood graining for the woodwork, and distemper for the walls. The precise date of execution is therefore unknown.

The painted ceiling in the Drawing Room is an example of the type of decoration common in more affluent country houses during the 18th and 19th centuries. This type of painting –

much of which would not have been carried out by a single artist but by a team of craftsmen using mass-produced stencils and patterns – falls somewhere between wall painting and interior decoration. Nonetheless, it is technically identical to a wall painting, and therefore the same techniques are required in its preservation. Moreover, the 'conserve as found' approach that has been taken to Brodsworth Hall is very much in keeping with the approach English Heritage has to the conservation of wall paintings generally: to record and preserve what remains without resorting to reconstruction.

Left, the Drawing Room; below left, detail of the Drawing Room ceiling; below, marbled decoration in the hall

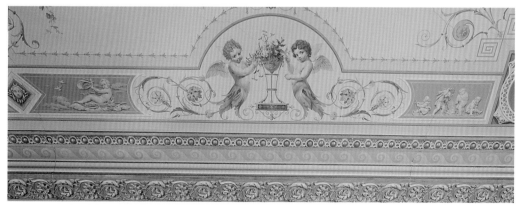

St Mary's Church, Studley Royal

The domed ceiling

William Burges (1827–1881) was one of the most prominent High Victorian architects working in the Gothic style during the latter half of the 19th century. His reputation attracted the attention of several wealthy patrons, among them the Marchioness of Ripon, who, in 1870, commissioned Burges to build two churches in memory of her son, Frederick Vyner. One of these was St Mary's Church at Studley Royal.

The church is a combination of early French and English Gothic styles. Its rich interior decoration and elaborate imagery are trademarks of Burges' work, and they reflect the family's deep religious sentiment. The focus of the decorative scheme is clearly the chancel, with the nave and side-aisles left relatively unadorned. With its elaborate stained glass, extensive mosaics on the floors and lower walls, and polished marble, this church has every inch of stone, timber, and metal painted and gilded with decorative and figurative work.

The scheme is meant to represent Paradise Lost and Paradise Regained, and to achieve this elaborate effect Burges' workshop prepared much of the materials – including stone, plaster casts, wood, canvas, and metal – in the studio. Craftsmen then applied or inserted the ready-prepared decoration, and finished the painting and gilding *in situ*. This workshop approach is typical of the Gothic revival popular during this period, and Studley Royal is certainly the consummate example of the Victorian Gothic style.

Richmond Castle

On the south side of the predominantly 12th-century castle at Richmond is a building which contains one of the most unusual pieces of wall decoration in English Heritage's collection. The 19th-century detention block, a building of eight cells located just inside the Castle entrance, held conscientious objectors during World War I. The walls of the cells within were the only place where the prisoners could record their personal and political beliefs, and what they have left behind – in the form of graffiti – is a poignant and unique survival.

These men – many of them Quakers, Congregationalists, Wesleyans, and Jehovah's Witnesses whose religious convictions would not allow them to fight – were conscripted into the army to join the non-combatant forces at Richmond and incarcerated when they refused to obey orders. In 1916, sixteen of the men were taken from the cells and subjected to punishment before being court martialled. Their sentence was death by firing squad, commuted to ten years' penal servitude.

The walls of Richmond Castle are fascinating testimony to the personal experiences of the prisoners. While awaiting their fate, they used the walls as their diaries to record their thoughts, draw images of their loved ones, or simply to count away the days. There are also later additions dating to World War II when the cells were apparently used as a punishment block for disorderly behaviour by soldiers, and then later still by visitors moved by the plight of earlier prisoners.

Technically, these are not wall paintings, in that they are not a form of intentional decoration and they are certainly not painted; in fact, in many cases they are just names or scrawls in pencil. Yet they are not crude graffiti either; there are many proficient drawings, including sketches of girlfriends (see back cover), political figures, and images of war. In terms of historical value they are an extremely important part of our history, and as a form of decoration made on limewash, just like many wall paintings, they are subject to the same principles of conservation.

Details of the graffiti

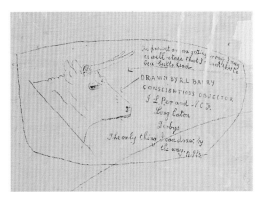

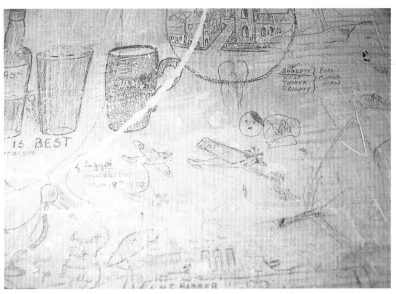

Chester Castle

19th-century engraving of the chapel

Above, the altar recess; right, detail of a man in a straw hat from an unidentified scene; opposite, the Bishop of Adana

The rediscovery of these 13th-century paintings must count as one of the most important 'finds' of medieval wall painting in England in recent years. Decoration had been recorded in the Agricola Tower of the castle as early as 1810 when an engraving was published of a scene on the west wall. In the 1920s, it was again recorded that 'the chapel had been covered with beautiful paintings'. However, by 1944–55, Professor Tristram's survey of medieval wall paintings only recorded 'traces of scroll ornament' on the chapel vault, and the paintings were assumed lost.

Then, during a routine inspection of the building in 1980 as part of the National Survey of Medieval Wall Painting, it was discovered that the altar recess was decorated with elegant busts of angels in roundels, extremely similar in style to 13th-century sculpture found in Westminster Abbey, done under the patronage of Henry III. As Chester Castle had been taken over by Henry in 1237, this then raised the exciting prospect that the paintings were part of a royal scheme of decoration, the only other one from this period being the fragmentary paintings in Windsor Castle.

In 1982, an investigation of the vault was undertaken, and one of the very first images to be found was an exquisite scene of the Visitation. More than 20 figures were found, as well as an inscription and ornamental decoration, all of which appear to have formed part of a cycle devoted to the Infancy of Christ. Fragmentary figure-subjects were also found on the upper parts of the chapel walls, thought to show the Miracles of the Virgin. Intriguingly, it was also discovered that earlier 12th-century decoration survived beneath the 13th-century paintings.

The excellent condition of the paintings is due to the durability of the original technique, which appears to be based on lime using a surprisingly limited range of pigments. Yet, despite the simplicity of technique, the paintings are of exceptional quality, their small scale reminiscent of contemporary stained glass and manuscript illumination. Although it is difficult to determine exactly when the paintings were executed, there are some indications that they may date to even earlier than 1237, ie to *c*1220, from the time of Earl Rannulf III. This could potentially be an even more exciting discovery than a royal scheme, since very little is known of baronial wall paintings of this period.

Belsay Castle

Above, detail of the Wild Man; right, detail of the ship

Upon entering the gloomy Great Hall in the picturesque ruin of Belsay Castle, the seemingly bare stone interior gives little away about the tastes of generations of Middleton family owners that lived there. While the thick stone walls of this northern 'tower-house' or 'pele' reflect justifiable concerns about defence on the northern borders, here in the principal room domestic luxury once predominated. Massive windows in the end walls, furnished with benches to enjoy the views, once lit a gaily painted interior. Remarkably, enough painting survives to reconstruct two medieval phases of decoration, each responding to contemporary fashion and together forming one of the most significant survivals of medieval secular painting in England.

As in every substantial building of its period, the 14th-century interiors at Belsay would originally have been painted. For the Great Hall at Belsay, the owners chose red vinescroll – a type of decoration made up of curling vines and leaves – against a bright white background. Second only to masonry pattern in popularity, vinescroll was typically used for large expanses of wall space and survives particularly well at Belsay in the splays of the windows. The painting was relatively quickly replaced by a far more ambitious decorative scheme in the 15th century.

This is divided into two tiers, with the upper level depicting a naval scene – perhaps an important event in the Middleton family history – with two ships and various figures. The lower tier consists of heraldic shields hanging from lopped trees set against a dark rolling landscape covered in clusters of white flowers with red centres, clearly referring to French *millefleurs*

tapestries of around 1460. But it was only during conservation work carried out by English Heritage in 1996 that an important discovery was made. Now only barely visible, a 'wild man' – a human figure covered with long hair – was found on the east wall. These figures commonly populated the margins of decorative schemes, often bearing shields, and at Belsay he is shown supporting a quartered shield of the Middleton and Strivelyn families.

It therefore seems that in the 15th century the entire room would have been divided into three horizontal tiers specifically designed to fit the shape of the room. A gently curved ceiling would have left space for four narrative pictures, such as the naval scene below, which was a huge expanse of painted imitation *millefleurs* tapestry with heraldry. The lowest tier, which retains faint traces of a three-dimensional chevron pattern, may have been covered with panelling or fabric.

Finchale Priory

It is said that Finchale, 'a wild and overgrown place, liable to floods and infested with poisonous snakes', was first inhabited by St Godric, who founded his hermitage here in 1115. Eventually, as Godric's reputation grew, a stone chapel was constructed, and after his death two monks were sent from Durham to occupy the site. By 1196, a monastery had been founded following a grant from Henry Puiset, son of the Bishop of Durham, and several Benedictine monks had settled here under the Prior of Finchale. The monastery grew and prospered, but the monastic buildings were not begun until about 1237, and were completed towards the end of the 13th century. The building was altered at the end of the 14th century.

One of the late 14th-century alterations to the building fabric was the walling-in of the Early English arcade in the east end of the nave. In 1925, when some of the piers on the south side of the nave were uncovered, a significant amount of painted decoration was revealed, preserved within the later stonework for nearly 600 years. According to early drawings made of the painting, it included a black, yellow, and red chevron ornament on a white ground, with decorative borders of circles and diamonds in black, red, and white.

The embedded column

Unfortunately, much of this painting is now lost, but traces of a chevron pattern on the first pier from the crossing and part of a roundel on the second pier are still visible. This survival is truly remarkable given that Finchale is a ruined site which is continuously exposed to the elements. It is also important evidence of the splendid decoration which once adorned the interiors of the great Benedictine monasteries – most of them sadly now in ruins – throughout the north of England.

Detail of the traces of painting

Further Reading

Conservation of wall paintings: proceedings of the international symposium on the conservation of wall paintings, 1979, Council for the Care of Churches, 1986

The conservation of English wallpaintings, being a report of a committee set up by the Central Council for the Care of Churches and the Society for the Protection of Ancient Buildings, Central Council for the Care of Churches, 1959

Babington, C, and Park, D, 'Uncovering medieval wall paintings in Chester Castle,' Minerva, vol 4, no 1, January/February 1993, 8–9

Caiger-Smith, A, English medieval mural paintings, Clarendon Press, Oxford, 1963

Cather, S (ed), The conservation of wall paintings: proceedings of a symposium organised by the Courtauld Institute of Art and the Getty Conservation Institute, London, 1987, Los Angeles, 1991

Croft-Murray, E, Decorative painting in England 1537–1837, 2 vols, 1962

Curteis, T, 'The Elizabethan wall paintings of Hill Hall: influences and techniques,' in Painting techniques: history, materials and studio practice, Contributions to the Dublin Congress, 7–11 September, 1998, IIC, London, 1998, 131–5

Davey, N, and Ling, R, Wall painting in Roman Britain, Britannia Monograph Series no 3, 1982

Demus, O, Romanesque mural painting, London, 1970

Gill, M, Manning, T, Park, D, and Stewart, S, 'The gatehouse wall painting: stylistic analysis,' Devon Archaeological Society, Proceedings, no 54, 1996: Berry Pomeroy Castle, Appendix 13, 317–23

Gill, M, 'Late medieval wall painting in England: content and context,' unpublished PhD thesis, Courtauld Institute of Art, London, 1998

Howard, H, Manning, T, and Stewart, S, 'Late medieval wall painting techniques at Farleigh Hungerford Castle and their context,' in Painting techniques: history, materials and studio practice, Contributions to the Dublin Congress, 7–11 September, 1998, IIC, London, 1998, 59–64

Keyser, C E, List of buildings…having mural…decorations, London, 1883

Lindley, P (ed), Gainsborough Old Hall, Occasional Papers in Lincolnshire History and Archaeology, 8, 1991

Ling, R, Romano-British wall painting, Shire Archaeology, Aylesbury, 1985

Mora, P, Mora, L, and Philippot, P, The conservation of wall paintings, London, 1984

Norton, C, and Park, D (eds), Cistercian art and architecture in the British Isles, Cambridge, 1986

Park, D, 'The Creation: marginalia and ornament in the refectory paintings of Bushmead Priory,' Bedfordshire Archaeology, vol 17, 1986, 72–6

Reader, F, 'Tudor domestic wall-paintings', part I, Archaeological Journal, 92, 1935, 243–86

Reader, F, 'Tudor domestic wall paintings', part II, Archaeological Journal, 93, 1936, 220–62

Reader, F, 'A classification of Tudor domestic wall paintings', part I, Archaeological Journal, 98, 1942, 181–211

Rickerby, S, 'Kempley: a technical examination of the Romanesque wall paintings,' in Cather, S, Park, D, and Williamson, P (eds), Early medieval wall painting and painted sculpture in England, Proceedings of a symposium at the Courtauld Institute of Art, February 1985, BAR British Series 216, 1990, 249–61

Rickerby, S, and Park, D, 'A romanesque Visitatio Sepulchri at Kempley,' The Burlington Magazine, no 1054, vol 133, January 1991, 27–31

Rickert, M, Painting in Britain: the Middle Ages, 2nd edition, 1965

Rouse, E C, Medieval wall paintings, 4th edition, Princes Risborough, 1991

Rouse, E C, and Baker, A, 'The wall-paintings at Longthorpe Tower, near Peterborough, Northants,' Archaeologia, 96, 1945

Thompson, D V, The materials and techniques of medieval painting, New York, 1956

Thompson, D V (trans), Cennino d'Andrea Cennini: The Craftsman's Handbook, New York, 1960

Tristram, E W, English medieval wall painting: the twelfth century, Oxford, 1944

Tristram, E W, English medieval wall painting: the thirteenth century, Oxford, 1950

Tristram, E W, English medieval wall painting: the fourteenth century, Oxford, 1955